CLICK RESET

WHY MINDSET, CHOICES AND FOCUS PLAY A SIGNIFICANT ROLE IN PRODUCTIVITY

ANTARA DEV

Dedicated to

All the exemplary achievers who made us realize that there are no limits to what one can achieve in this world.

Contents

Contents

Foreword

Every once in a while we discuss at Finology, are we doing the right thing? Are we moving in the right direction? What can we do better? This process of questioning ourselves, always trying to find the best solution, and always looking for ways to improve our process has taken us where we are today. The same applies in life. If we keep moving ahead with the productivity practices taught by our parents, or by ten people we are surrounded with, we will end up achieving the same results as they have. Instead of that, why not learn the best practices used by experts and successful people. This book is going to solve that problem. If your goal is to casually pass through it, you can drop the effort of reading it. But if you want to live your best self, set your intentions to deliberately practice the ideas shared in Click Reset.

This book deserves a place in every home and office. It's a book you must refer to anytime you feel you are unproductive. Consider it your personal productivity guide. It teaches you how to develop the right mindset for success, what are the most effective productivity choices, and how your life depends on what you focus.

Every time I meet with Antara, I instantly feel a connection with her because of her relentless urge to seek the right answer. Be it productivity, spirituality, nutrition, she is on it. Her unending quest in exploring the bests of life, her passion for productivity, and her perfectionist attitude towards work, all can be experienced through this book.

Personally for me clicking reset means daring to think different, daring to go beyond what is told to us. The rebel from normal, ordinary, usual, is what I call clicking reset in life.

Every year twenty lacs students appear for the CBSE exam. They study the same course, they memorize the same answers. What are we trying to do, are we trying to manufacture clones? I think it's time, we click reset on the default mode of operation. I think it's time India's youth take charge of their future. Do not let the fear of "What if I fail?" haunt you. Rather, fear what if I am just similar to others.

The methodologies shared in Click Reset are real and well tested. This book is full of research-backed ideas. The well-curated workbook and chapter-end action challenges will help you fasten your efforts. Let this book guide you in your daily choices. Let it shake your beliefs about yourself. Let it guide you in choosing your most productive habits.

Pranjal Kamra
Entrepreneur, author, and a Youtuber

Acknowledgements

My gratitude to all the researchers, writers, and productivity experts of the world. Without your knowledge and experience, this book would not have been possible.

I am eternally grateful to all the readers who know "they have what it takes; who are willing to challenge themselves and are ready to level up."

I cannot thank Harshit Pandey enough for encouraging me to write this book. If he had not continuously told me to write it myself, I would still have thought that I cannot even write a paragraph myself. Thank you for showing me my true capabilities.

Deepak Varadadi held my hand when I needed it the most. His stupendous command over language and ingenious imagination helped me present my concepts beautifully. He diligently added beauty to every paragraph I wrote.

Special thanks to Amaan Ahmed for reviewing my book with explicit honesty and utmost dedication. Without his comments on each line, this book could not have met my expectations.

Deepak and Amaan cushioned the pressure one faces in the initial stages of book writing. I am grateful to have you two on my team.

Jay Dewangan guided me in the initial stages of book writing. He made me realize how important it is for a writer to be able to convey her thoughts with clarity. A book may have amazing ideas, but if a reader cannot grasp them, it is nothing. His advice made me simplify my writing style.

Thank you, Saptarshi Das, Anushka Dave, and Amitabh Agrawal for agreeing to check my draft and making fastidious corrections. If something has escaped their eyes, consider it my mistake. It's said, no matter how many rounds of checking are done in a book, some mistakes can always be there.

Thank you to my dear cousin Palash Dewangan for saying yes to the crazy idea of writing a book on productivity. By laying the foundation, he made my job much easier. My acknowledgment would not be complete without a special thanks to my mother who filled a little girl's mind with dreams. She always made me imagine myself as a strong bold lady. And my wise father always encouraged me to up-skill. This combination of one telling me to fly high and the other reminding me of how much I am yet to achieve, made me who I am today.

Prologue

Every time I come across this question, "How do some people achieve so much in the same twenty-four hours," I cannot find a particular answer. Indeed, the truth is, there is no single reason behind it. Peak performance doesn't surface in a person due to discipline or intelligence. Superachievers do a lot of other things right to achieve their feat. This book is written to bring forth the precepts for massive performance. It's written to take you a step closer towards your goals. It's written because none of us are taught what it takes to be successful in our mother's womb.

Results become inevitable when we focus on doing little things right. A lot in our life becomes easy when we know the right way to do it. "Click Reset and Do It Right" will give you a level playing ground by unfolding the aspects that can 10X your productivity. It will list down the precepts for massive performance and will transform your working style as you read through it.

No matter which path of life we walk in, what goals we have, deep down in our hearts, we all seek the very best for ourselves. But will the best version be made itself? Perhaps not. Perhaps it appears only to those who seek it. It requires a conscious attempt towards finding the undiscovered side of oneself. It requires a deliberate effort to be ready to Click Reset whenever necessary and start afresh in the right way.

In the haphazardness of life, we have forgotten that there can be an altogether different hidden side of all of us. A side that we are not aware of, neither dreamt of nor thought of—a side hidden with numerous plausible stories. I wonder how incredible that unrevealed side would look, and will everyone ever get the chance to see it? Largely no! Because some treasures get revealed only to those who believe in its presence.

This book contains a barrage of secrets to improve your performance, without which, there will always be scope for improvement. When practiced, these small action-oriented decisions promise to help you achieve extraordinary results in a short period. But let me put this straight. To reap the benefits, it would require a paradigm shift. If you read this book with the wrong mindset you have been carrying for years, you will be able to reap a mere ten percent of the results. To make the most of it, you need to unlearn certain myths and be coachable. Look at it with a fresh perspective, and it will do wonders. Be willing to adapt to the right mindset, and it will alter your reality. With the right mindset, I mean, you need to be willing to learn, improve, and implement. You need to have the desire to beat your records and a deep urge to tap your full potential. I am saying this because I know you have it. No matter what you do, where you are in your life, you have it in you. You only need to be willing to tap into it.

It's no fun to live in mediocrity. Living a life without limitations has its own flavor. Our limitations destroy the beauty of life. Sadly, we are always told to settle for average, dream within our realities, within our constraints, to define our potential not much beyond our current capabilities. Rarely are we suggested to stretch our boundaries. Physical barriers are easy to fight as you are aware of them. Mental barriers are intangible. Deep inside our minds, we have created limitations, and we have trained ourselves to plant seeds within them. But why do we do it? Why do we happily create these limitations? That's because our brains are wired to protect us. The brain's limbic system that consists of glands like amygdalae, hypothalamus, and other structures is responsible for emotions and memory formation. This region of the brain is most commonly associated as the emotion receptor, which gets activated when we are provoked.

Our brain likes certainty. When it comes across vagueness, it feels vulnerable and alerts us for the dangers ahead. This feeling of vulnerability is what causes fear inside us. Fear of change, fear of uncertainty, and fear of failure occurs because our brain learns by pattern recognition. The more repetition it sees, the more comfortable it gets. If all of a sudden you give it a new experience, it does not know what to do with it. Sometimes it even gets afraid of it. This is the reason why in general we are unable to break our boundaries. As most of us are fed with wrong information about our capabilities. We have fed our brain wrong signals of dangers, triggering its fight or flight response mechanism. We have been told that change is bad, failure is bad, challenges aren't good and thus have made ourselves fearful of them. However, fear is merely a prediction of danger made by our brain. The presence of fear doesn't mean that the outcome will be bad.

The human brain processes information the same way machine learning functions in the technological world. It learns from the continuous source of data it receives. When we feed our brain failure as an outcome, it starts believing so. When we feed our brain success as an outcome, it perceives it as the same. By merely changing our thoughts, we can change our brain's working mechanism. However, for ages, we have been feeding our DNA continuous signals of danger. Our ancestors lived in forests surrounded by wild animals. They had to be vigilant of all possible risks. They kept their eyes wide open. Any tiny signal of danger released their stress hormone triggering their flight or fight response. Glad it worked in that format; otherwise, the human species would have been extinct by now.

However, in today's scenario, we do not need to be watchful of dangers. We do not need to be afraid of wild animals. Still, we have a DNA that responds to the tiniest of fears. This fear is so severe that it has brought limitations even in our dreams. For each of us, our dream house has different amenities and choices of the locality. Rarely do we find people imagining a dream house massively different from their current capabilities. Our imagination is a function of our surroundings. Even when a man imagines his dream house having double the amenities of his existing home, he never imagines it too far from his reality. It makes absolute sense to be more realistic than optimistic, but let's accept reality has its restrictions. And the question you must ask is, are these restrictions serving your life's purpose?

How would you feel if we get the power to alter reality? Sounds terrific, right? To some of us, it's like taking birth in an entirely new scenario, going to a completely different school and college, and getting numerous good opportunities. Well, what has happened has happened, and it cannot be changed, but whether we believe it or not, we do have the power to reorient our future. Then why don't we do it? Why don't we take action to build a new reality? Why don't we think of molding it by 1000%?

Are we too lazy?

No.

Are we too ignorant?

Maybe.

Don't we think it's possible?

We know it is possible.

Then what's the problem?

The problem is we are too afraid to take the big step.

We are afraid because we know that big steps would require some real actions, some substantial changes in our choices, habits, work-related decisions, relationships, and more than all of that, in our mindset. Doing is easy when your mindset is right. The challenging part is to take the right step towards building an apt mindset.

But why are we afraid to take that step?

Because we have already defined our capabilities somewhere in the back of our mind, which may not necessarily be true. Mostly, it's untrue, yet, many of us prove it right.

Ever wondered why it has always proven to be right?

It's because we never tried to question it. We followed them diligently, and what we have followed has become our reality.

When we were born, we were born like any other child. What we have consciously and subconsciously brought into our existence is what we have become today. We were all born equal, but today we are not the same. So what changed in between? I agree that the city we are born in matters. The religion we are born in makes a difference. But keeping that aside, two kids born in the same religion, the same neighborhood, are still different. We are basically an outcome of our mindset and choices. If we want to change ourselves, we need to alter them. We need to reset them and start again with the right ones.

There's a difference between knowing the truth and following it. How many people do you know in your surroundings who have read the Bible, Gita, or Quran? I think each one of us knows someone who has read these scriptures. If you live in India, it's quite impossible to escape Gita, Ramayana, and Mahabharata's learnings. Some people have read it twice, and some have read it about ten times. For those who believe, the teachings in these books have the power to transform their lives in a day!

Norman Vincent Peale, a physician and the author of the famous book "The Power of Positive Thinking," discussed numerous instances in his book on how the verses of the Bible have changed the lives of thousands of people and his patients. Do you think these people hadn't read the Bible before they were suggested by him? There's a good chance many of them did read it. Then why didn't it work before but later? What changed in between? People's faith and receptivity. We are always surrounded by good ideas but are unable to perceive them because we are not fully attuned to them. Many have read these scriptures and know that negative emotions such as ego, jealousy, anger, revenge, guilt, regret, etc. are humans' biggest enemies. But how many of them do you think live by what they have read? Today, it's well accepted that most of our diseases are triggered by stress and emotional illnesses. Yet, people don't give it the attention it deserves. These negative emotions aren't just depriving humans of their happiness, but it's also forfeiting their lives. These emotions aren't considered negative because they harm others. They are considered negative because they harm you.

The book in your hand is full of ideas and techniques on how to be more productive and make the most use of your energy. Do not ignore the research-backed productivity enhancers discussed here. Form an opinion only after you try them. Part one of the book solely focuses on developing your subconscious. Part two and three contain direct giveaways to bring immediate results. The book is substituted with ready-to-use exercises to be filled as and when directed in the chapters. All the chapters contain an action challenge at the end to help you install the learnings immediately.

To become a master, one must practice with the tools every day. The techniques and ideas provided here are the techniques you must use repeatedly to improve your productivity; until it becomes second nature. If you promise to be receptive, I promise to deliver you the best. You need not follow the book completely. Depending on your situation, follow the precepts you think can bring a difference in your life. But before you decide what precepts have more value for you, you need to see it with a clear mind, without biases, and with belief.

Why do we need to click reset?

Scientists have discovered a child's subconscious is developed before he turns eight. Until then, a child's brain downloads the data from its surroundings. This data works as software that runs the rest of his life. Neuroscientists have revealed that ninety-five percent of our life is run by our subconscious. Only five percent is run by our conscious mind. That says our subconscious accounts for almost every activity we do. Indeed, our subconscious mind is many times faster than our conscious mind. And thus, it easily manipulates our conscious brain into following its paths. This explains why it is so tough to convince people to do something entirely out of their way. We keep convincing their conscious brain when their subconscious takes all the decisions.

The subconscious mind runs in the background and makes a note of everything. When it gets exposed to similar information often, it adjusts itself and accepts the excessively exposed information as a fact. That's one reason why negative talks and positive affirmations both work. If you want to alter your subconscious, all you need to do is repeatedly expose it to the same information. After a point, your subconscious will accept the idea. Exactly how you form a habit through repetitiveness and form your beliefs from what you continuously learn from your surroundings instead of facts.

John B. Watson, the father of behaviorism, states that "Give me a dozen healthy infants, well-formed, and my own specified world to bring them up in and I'll guarantee to take anyone random and train him to become any type of specialist I might select- doctor, lawyer, artist, merchant-chief and, yes, even beggar-man and thief, regardless of his talents, penchants, tendencies, abilities, vocations, and race of his ancestors." Human behavior can be modified through conditioning: a behaviorist mechanism that uses continuous reinforcement of the response or stimulus. This mechanism is typically used to train animals. Although humans are not a part of deliberate conditioning, they naturally condition themselves into individual behavior as per the reward and penalties they get on a day to day basis. The stubbornness of a child is a simple example of reward and penalty. Kids learn early that their parents would agree to their wants if they keep insisting. If one-day parents stop agreeing to their demands no matter how much they hang on to their idea, they stop doing it, realizing there's no reward for their effort. Almost all of our behavior is based on rewards and penalties we have experienced. We have always got some reward in being the way we are, whether in the form of happiness, recognition, power, etc., or in the form of less effort, fun, relaxation, etc.

Right from our childhood, we are getting shaped by the beliefs and habits of our family members, relatives, neighbors, friend circle; people we follow; content we consume, and the books we read. They are unceasingly shaping our thoughts and responses regardless of our will. We are a result of what we get exposed to. Indubitably, this exposure can only contort our ideologies but cannot handicap our capabilities. Our potential doesn't depend on our surroundings. It depends on us. It depends on what we decide to do with our body, mind, and soul. A man who is willing to break this barrier can be stopped by none. The only basic requirement is his willingness, along with the handy tools.

CLICK RESET puts forth the precepts that will redefine the way you work. It will show you ways to reset your style, thought process, and beliefs and will help you start again with the precepts of productivity. It will help you do things in the way it's meant to be done and open up several new choices that can elevate your performance. Knowing what to do is not enough. How we do it can bring a significant difference. We have done many things wrong but have expected the right results. To not get sidelined, we need to know the obvious.

Productivity is massively dependent on three aspects: Your mindset, your choices, and your ability to focus. Your mindset is a potent extract of your subconscious mind. Your choices are picked by your conscious brain. And your ability to focus determines how efficiently you get things done. Mindset and choices are interlinked as until you build the right mindset, you wouldn't be able to make the most use of daily productive choices, and until you make good choices, you would not be able to formulate the right mindset. The combination of the right mindset and the right choices, along with unwavering focus, can give you your most productive self.

To find out your current level of productivity, refer to Part 1 - "Bird's eye view of your productivity" of the Workbook.

Right Mindset

All successful people have one factor in common: they have the right mindset for success. Give them anything, and they would thrive in it. The probability of success might fall or rise depending on their interest, but the attitude with which they take up every challenge doesn't change. Their effort, proactiveness, willpower, competitiveness, focus, confidence, decision-making ability, and determination never takes a toll irrespective of what they do. They have developed those qualities, and no situation can snatch it away from them. It's this self-training of years that has pushed them towards riches.

When I was a child, I wondered why doesn't the government take up all the wealth of the country and split it into the population equally? I thought that the problem of poverty would get solved if that happens. Everyone will be happy, and nobody will have to suffer. Then why doesn't the government do that? Is it too much of a process to go through, or is it because they can't convince the rich people? For some while, I felt nobody thought of this because it would be unfair to those who accumulated wealth, and there would be complete disagreement from wealthy people for the same. Though I wasn't wrong in my thinking, the more understanding I gained, the more I realized that it isn't the sole reason. The truth was harsher than what I had imagined early. I realized that the fact is, even if we distribute the wealth of the nations equally in their population, within no time, it will get back to those from which it came. It's the mindset of the people that define what they do with their money. Even when someone wins a lottery, their mindset takes them back to where they were before within a few years. Possibly they would have bought their dream house or had gone for vacation, but rarely did someone try to make it multi-fold. Sadly, the question of how they can do it also doesn't arise in their mind. It's this mindset that makes all the difference.

Interestingly, every year the riches by way of philanthropy give away approximately two percent of US GDP. Though that's not enough, that's not a small amount either. The world made total philanthropy of $427 billion in 2018. That's more than the GDP of South Africa, the UAE, Singapore, Hong Kong, Israel, and many other nations.

Many people are willing to improve others' lives by donating money directly to them. They avoid doing it because they know the money will not solve their problem. It can give temporary relief, but it wouldn't change things dramatically for most of them. Some governments have already tried and failed. Indeed, there are many cases in Indian families where one subset of the family earns well, and the other doesn't. Out of love, the well-to-do family members give away a good sum of money to stabilize the not so blessed family members. Yet, rarely do we see it helping them transform their lives. Some people even help their relatives set up a business, but that doesn't always bear fruits as they expected. At times, we do see some contrasting stories. These stories originate where the receiver also has the caliber to make a difference with this help. That caliber is what I call the right mindset for success. The mindset that helps you to do the right thing, the right way at the right time!

This use of the right mindset does not just apply to the creation of wealth, but it also applies to success in relations, happiness, and health and, in short, to different definitions of success for different people. Of course, the mindset alone can't bring you various riches of life, bad luck can always take a toll, but it will surely build the ability to face situations. The beautiful thing about the right mindset is, it always takes you forward. It works as a potent force in running your life and ultimately takes you to a place where you are better off than where you were yesterday. When you know there are only advantages to having it, why not deliberately develop it?

Choices

Did you ever find that some of your friends are ahead of you, despite being less intelligent, less resourceful, and less hard-working than you are? Have you had the chance to sneak-peak into their routine? What do they do differently? It can be one activity or a combination of activities. They may not be intelligent, but their choices can be. Believe it or not, their small choices have brought them a huge difference from the rest of the crowd. Despite starting from a level playing ground, simple choices like following a good lifestyle or finding a mentor have brought them advantages over others. Your productivity has a lot of its dependence on your habits and choices. Some are universally accepted, but many are still hidden from people. Some choices may have been belittled by most of us, but their significance can't be forgotten. We can't realize the importance until we try and experience the differences.

Your ability to focus

More often than not, ideas worth billions cross our minds. But why doesn't it materialize? Because it crosses the mind of a person who lacks the desire to execute it. It appears in the mind of a person who lacks the courage to drop the fear of failure and jump on it. It knocks on the door of a person who doesn't have faith in his ideas, nor is he ready with the skills required. Remember, courage can be built, skills can be acquired, and faith can be generated. But desire has to come from within. If an idea mixes with desire, it gets the genius to invent it. If you have all of the above, the only thing you need is FOCUS!

Legends do not become legends because they do too many things well. They become legends because they learn to do a specific thing better than anyone else. They choose the thing they want to fight for and stick with it. They find the factor that deserves their maximum attention and put every bit of energy into it. They may face similar problems as we all face, but they keep themselves focused. To them, where the world is going doesn't matter. The only thing that matters is their journey and their destination.

To build focus, you have to sideline anything and everything that comes between you and your destination. When you are on your road to success, prepare to cut back ninety-nine percent of the things you come across, including your less desirable dreams and your dearest family members.

Don't drink it. Chew it!

To be honest, most people aren't looking to do the hard work; they simply want to get more things done. They are waiting for things that can inspire them to get into action. They are like, "Give me something I can drink right away that can make me successful." That's not possible. You may rely on motivational videos or some source of information that has inspired you in the past and include it in your routine to get yourself moving every day. But to do that, you still need to do things and take action yourself. There is nothing anyone can do to make you move. No one apart from you has control over your conscious mind, responsible for moving your body parts. People may give you fabulous ideas, but you have to make an effort.

I wish you luck in your endeavors, and I hope every part of this book helps you build your future.

"May the best day of your past be the worst day of your future."

An Irish Blessing

MINDSET

CHAPTER ONE

WATCH YOUR THOUGHTS

A man may be a product of his thoughts, but thoughts are often the product of the environment. The "bully a plant" experiment conducted by IKEA in 2018 stands up for it. In a UAE school, IKEA placed two identical plants in separate glass chambers with the same ecological conditions. Students bullied one plant verbally and boosted the other one with compliments. The comments were recorded and played continuously to the plants. After thirty days, the results were visible. The plant which received compliments flourished while the plant that heard insults wilted.

Dr. Masaru Emoto performed a similar experiment on the effect of words, prayers, music, and the environment on water's molecular structure. He filled water in different glass bottles and stuck a note to each of them with terms like sad, happy, guilt, gratitude, and regret. He then froze the water bottle and examined the resulting crystals' aesthetic properties under microscopic photography. The results were remarkable. The photographs from the bottles exposed to positive words had beautiful crystal formations. The pictures from the bottles exposed to negative terms showed haphazard malformed constructions. He performed similar experiments to find the effect of different music and prayers on water. The results were identical. [1.1]

Another interesting story comes out from Solomon Island. Some reports say that if a tree in Solomon Island is too big to be logged with an ax, a group of people yell on it every day for a few hours. They call it "Curse Magic." Within a month, the tree dies and falls off. The tree's life energy gets damaged by cursing and slowly kills it from the inside.

Ever since we are born, we have been an offspring of the circumstances we grew up in. Our surroundings have an impact on our habits, our behavior, and our thoughts. Even our mood, current perspective, or general outlook towards a stimulus is a direct result of what's been happening around us. Our energy levels, our belief system, and our productivity is heavily influenced by the things we are surrounded with. The type of movies and TV shows we watch, the people we interact with, the kind of information we expose ourselves to, and the quality of our internal and external conversations, all of it influences our mentality. If plants and water can get affected by it, imagine the impact it has on our lives.

Though it's hard to believe and measure the effect these small things have on all living beings, somewhere we know it can't be a lie. Even a tiny constructive criticism from a close friend makes us feel dejected. Ponder the impact, a negative thought ungrained in us since our childhood can create. Most of the thoughts and beliefs a person has are offsprings of an event of their early childhood. In any life transformation course, the central focus revolves around clearing the unnecessary thoughts and beliefs in people's minds. They do it by helping them get aware of their beliefs and by making them realize that it has no relevance today. Most of our beliefs get formed in early childhood however, they take a toll on us throughout our lives. Don't you agree? Try this-

1. Close your eyes. Sit in a comfortable position. Relax your body. Breathe deeply for two to three minutes and become aware of every part of your body. Pay close attention to every breath you take in and give out. Become mindful of your face, shoulders, chest, arms, waist, thighs, calves, and toes.

2. Think of a strong belief you have, think as deep as you can, and see when was the first time you felt the way you feel about it now. Keep thinking. You will soon find an answer and the reason behind your belief. Find the first instance when this belief was ingrained in your mind. Look as closely as possible.

I hope you have discerned the moment your belief started to form its way into your subconscious. Now, since you are more aware of how that belief came into existence and the circumstances in which it originated, you have the power to change how you feel about it. Your past belief originated because of a circumstance that originated in your past, which does not exist today. Living your life carrying the old belief, which has no relevance today, is mistreatment to self. Learn not to be a victim of it by being watchful of your thoughts and their origin.

One way to get rid of it is through listening to your inner voice. Your beliefs talk to you. They remind you what you think of a person when they are around. They quickly tell you how you shall behave with them. It goes the same in the case of events and circumstances. You act in a certain way unknowingly due to the experiences you had in the past. Despite the change of scenario, your brain keeps reminding you of the past and directs you to act in a certain way. Catch yourself every time you hear your mind speak to you. It tells you a lot about your beliefs. Practice to question the voice and dig deep to find the reason it originated. This technique not just helps you to know yourself better, but it also gives you the chance to modify your perceptions. It lets you rethink your ideas and reframe your ideologies.

We form memories when there are emotions attached to it. Without the presence of strong emotions, memory formation is not possible. Our beliefs and ideologies are a result of layers of memory. But our general attitude gets shaped by the current scenarios.

Action Challenge: Eliminate an unnecessary feeling/behavior. Following are the steps:

1. Write down a specific emotion/behavior you want to get rid of. Example: Anger, Regret, Drinking Habit, etc.

2. Find the factor/person responsible for it. Example: Specific reason/ behavior that makes you angry/regretful, friend circle, mini bar at home, etc.

3. Take immediate steps to eliminate the factor. Example: Start meditating to control your anger, say I forgive my mistakes in the front of the mirror every day, spend more time with like-minded people. Steps you would take:

CHAPTER TWO

DEVELOP THE ATMOSPHERE FOR PRODUCTIVITY

Christine Porath and Christine Pearson polled thousands of workers for fourteen years from various industries on their experience of receiving uncivil treatment. Half of the workers said they were treated rudely at least once a week and ninety-eight percent claimed to have experienced discourteous behavior at work. [2.1] That's a considerable number. Even if we believe the figure is exaggerated and only half of it is true, that still means 49% of the workers strongly experienced a treatment they didn't like.

Humans may forget the stories, but they always remember the feelings they had to go through. The feeling stays in the memory and reminds us again and again of those hurtful moments. And one would be wrong to think these memories do not impact our work ethic. Research shows that most people are unproductive when they are stressed, unhappy, or demotivated. When your spirits are high, you might even be willing to help out your colleague at work. But when you're gloomy, you would probably procrastinate on your own work. A good mood is very pivotal, indeed.

Another poll conducted on eight hundred managers and employees from different industries shared that, among the workers receiving uncivil treatment, forty-eight percent intentionally decreased their work effort, forty-seven percent intentionally decreased the time spent at work, and seventy-eight percent said that their commitment to the organization declined.

Most of us work in a team, either with our superiors, subordinates, or our peers. The impact of one's behavior isn't limited to the receiver. It also impacts the action of the people witnessing it. I am sure you can think of someone you slightly dislike not because of their behavior towards you but because of their behavior towards someone else. Humans are emotional and keen observers. They love the goodness that gets spread and hate the unmanly behavior. Consciously or unconsciously, they try to disassociate with bad people. Hence, it's essential to foster an environment that depresses discourteous behavior and encourages positivity. Create an environment both in home and offices that encourages positive feedback, constructive criticism, autonomy, cooperativeness, and humanly treatment we all deserve.

In some offices, pressure flows like air. It has become a part of their culture. Though some people tend to perform better under pressure. But that doesn't imply that stress is beneficial for them. They perform better because they have learned to develop robust psychological skills to handle the pressure. When a person perceives pressure as a challenge, he tends to cope well. When he perceives pressure as a threat, it hinders his productivity. Unfortunately, most people perceive pressure as a threat rather than as a challenge. Build an environment that encourages goal-setting without threatening employees' job security.

A positive environment has its significance in personal relations as well. Those kids who have a soothing home environment flourish more easily than those who are regularly a part of a hostile environment. Most parents try to raise a child they want, not a child they have. Resultantly they instill anxiety, low morale, and a cantankerous attitude in their kids. Neutral parenting, i.e., neither positive nor negative, is always in the child's best interest. That's because negative thoughts are four to seven times more potent than positive thoughts.[2.2] And only giving positive comments to your child can discourage their progress.

In her book "Mindset: The New Psychology of Success," Carol Dweck explains, those kids whose parents and teachers foster a growth mindset perform much better and are always ready for the challenge than kids with a fixed mindset. With the growth mindset, she meant fostering the ability to willfully take up new challenges, not getting discouraged with failures, and taking every experience as a learning experience. People with a growth mindset think they can be good at anything by putting in the effort. While people with a fixed mindset believe that talent is innate and practice cannot change their feat.

Do you know a person who has achieved some incredible stuff and seems to you like a superhuman? My friend Amaan Ahmed reminds me of that. He might seem like a gifted child to some, but he is one of the perfect examples of the growth mindset. Before he turned nineteen, he knew how to fly a helicopter, handle venomous snakes and crocodiles, been a part of surgery done on various wild animals like lions and tigers, and had read more than 2500 books, including 600 encyclopedias. When I asked him how he learned to do so much, he said, "I go by the idea of learning enough to be capable of doing things well. I want to learn it, and so I do it." When I further asked him, "Don't you ever feel that you can't do it?" He immediately said, "No." Finding me perplexed with his reply, he said, "I think I can do everything, keeping in mind the practical aspect in terms of financial and operational feasibility." He shared he never tries to be the best at something. He tries to do it well and enjoys the experience of learning. This boy perfectly resembles the growth mindset. He enjoys the learning experience but never plays to be a winner. His mother is undoubtedly someone to be given credit for what she has inculcated in him, a growth mindset. She taught him, "he can do it" by encouraging him to learn and not win. She praised him lightly with words like "Nice" and "Well done." She didn't overdo it like most of us do. She understands child psychology and thus very well knows the must and mustn't of parenting.

Whenever it comes to encouraging someone, don't overdo it. Whether it's your employees, children, or partner. Encourage them with light comments. Ofcourse, never be ignorant. Praise them, but don't do it so much that they feel they have achieved everything.

Also don't be ignorant of the impact our negative comments have on the people around us. We mindlessly say things, thinking, it will get the people to do what we want, but the results aren't fruitful. When you need to be straight or convey a negative message to someone, I request you to take a step back and see if you can gently give the same message without discouraging the receiver.

In the short book, "The one minute manager," the author explains that one trick to be a great manager is to catch people doing something right. Yes, he meant right, not wrong. Most of us try to catch people doing something terrible to get the chance to tell them to do it better and faster. But the problem with that attitude is that when we catch people doing something bad, they feel dejected and demotivated. And we bear the pressure to inform them and correct them. However, when we catch people doing good, it encourages them to do better naturally without the effort of praising.

Dr. Bruce Lipton, a famous American biologist, says, "A minimum of one-third of all medical intervention is a placebo effect. That's the result of positive thinking". He also shares that the nocebo effect is "equally powerful with affecting your biology as is positive thinking, but it works in the opposite direction." [2.3] Our thoughts impact the behavior of fifty trillion cells in our body. Each cell of our body is present with an intent. It receives its instruction not only from our genes but also from our energetic environment. Every negative thought that crosses our mind disturbs our cells' harmony, while every positive thought brings it back.[2.4] You will be aghast to know that researchers have agreed that more than seventy percent of our thoughts are negative and repetitive. If that train of thought doesn't get eliminated or replaced with positive ones, we will not perform in our best forms.

For massive productivity, learn to create happy supporting surroundings, whether at home or in the office. Simple changes in how you interact with others, the comments you pass, your tone, your smile, and your inner talks can bring huge differences in your life and the lives of people around you. The energy you radiate to others is what comes back to you. The thoughts you accumulate in your mind have the power to alter your behavior.

Action Challenge: For the next one week:

1. Pay attention to the comments you are passing.

2. Neither discourage nor overly encourage someone. use comments like: good, nice, keep it up, you can do better, etc.

CHAPTER THREE

BE AT THE RIGHT PLACE

Have you ever wondered why students graduating from top institutions like MIT, Yale, Oxford, Harvard, and Princeton are one of the most successful? Hold your horses! I know you would say they are talented in the first place to get admitted into such prestigious institutions. And that surely is the truth, but it's not the complete story. Every student in such institutions is individually talented. However, it is the company of many such equally or maybe better-talented people that has led to their transformation. The faculty could be right, the infrastructure could be excellent, the resources could be vast, and everything about these institutions could be just perfect. But above all of it, these institutions get to flair well because it is the place where the best talents come under one roof to display their skills. Even if you put an average random student in any of these institutions, there's a high chance he would turn out to be successful. He wouldn't be successful because he would be learning through the best resources and teachers. He would be successful because of the exemplary surroundings he would seize.

Our surroundings have a massive impact on our being. Scientists have discovered that our subconscious mind gets developed in the initial eight years, including the time spent in our mother's womb. The things we see and learn from our surroundings build our subconscious, which plays a significant role in shaping our thinking patterns in the later years. From the conversations we have, the clothes we wear, the food we eat, to the values we have, all of it is given by the people around us. It's evident in our inclination towards certain actors, TV series, and movies. We seldom get to save ourselves from our best friend's choices. Most of the time, their favorites end up becoming our favorite. Those people who have strong convictions behind their choices also have them because of their past circumstances. Their surroundings created their thoughts and beliefs.

Whether we agree or not, the people we surround ourselves with profoundly affect our psychology. Our self-talks, our outlook towards life, our work efficiency, our goals, and our dreams are deep in our minds getting shaped by these people. Since it's, in turn, shaping our future self and us, it's critical that we gauge its effect and not fall prey to them.

Let me give you an example. I have been postponing exercise for the last eight years. I saved my old slim fit clothes for like five years, hoping it would fit me someday. I kept buying new slim-fit clothes, trusting that eventually, I will get in shape. Yet, I did not start exercising. I finally lost hope and started buying practical loose-fit outfits, realizing that I would never find time to exercise. But then I became friends with a man who is a fitness freak. As we started hanging out together, within a month, my eating habits, activity level, and simple choices like taking stairs instead of an elevator started to change. Soon I started exercising daily. Now, it's been a year since I met him, and I can proudly say that I am in a position to wear all my slim fits. I have lost 22 pounds to this date, and I am sure I will lose some more. That's the power our surroundings have on us.

American entrepreneur, author, and motivational speaker Jim Rohn says, "You are the average of five people you spend the most time with." The five people around you influence your income, lifestyle choices, habits, and almost everything about you. When you change these people around you, you change yourself. Always choose your friends, thoughtfully. They do not just represent you. They shape you.

But how do we decide who these five people should be?

Eleanor Roosevelt has the answer. The social activist and former First Lady says, "Great minds discuss ideas; average minds discuss events; small minds discuss people." The quote itself says a lot. It can be used as one of the guiding principles to evaluate your conversations and, thereby, the people around you. Once you start observing, you will notice that those who discuss ideas radiate positive energy. In contrast, those who discuss people shed negativity.

Many times, we needlessly become part of unconstructive conversations. In such a circumstance, the best approach is to nod and divert the topic. If you can, be blunt about disliking it. It does sound too much, but at times that's what the other one needs to hear. All the more, you are making it clear that you don't support meaningless conversations. If it persists, reduce your connection.

Evaluate whether the people in your surrounding have the same goals as you have? Find out the impact your inner circle is having on you. Assess the positives and negatives you are deriving from these relationships. Weigh up the percentage of the traits you would be happy to have from your friends. If it is above, say seventy percent, you are probably surrounded by the right people. But what if it is below forty percent? If it's clear that being with them has more negative effects on your life than positive, it's time to change your company. Spend less time with these people. Look for people who are heading in the same direction as you are. Be with people who are positively impacting you, already have the qualities you want, and take you closer to your goals.

After selling Paypal, Elon Musk shifted to Los Angeles. Though he had no idea what he wanted to do in the space industry, he moved to the city because he wanted to be in the company of the aeronautics industry's best scientists. He thought he would be able to refine his ideas if he would be around like-minded people. He attended events by Mars Society and soon joined it as its board of directors and later started his company SpaceX.

He made a similar move by shifting to Canada when he was seventeen. He knew, to become successful, he had to go to the United States. At that time, Canada seemed a more accessible option as he had many relatives in the city.

Elon Musk isn't the only one making these bold choices. The whole silicon valley is filled with such examples. The same people who find it tough to build a start-up somewhere else in the country, move to silicon valley because they know how their environment can impact their businesses. They know what it means to have the right resources, the right talent, and passion around them.

Many of us fall back on these little steps that can change our life. Some people resort to their ego and think they can achieve everything from wherever they are. I am not encouraging you to change your city, but I surely recommend choosing your surroundings wisely. And before you do that, be mentally prepared to radiate the same level of energy as your new community is radiating. Otherwise, why would someone let you come closer? Be willing and capable of giving as much as you are getting.

Also remember, it's tough to bring in great people in your life without reducing your bond with others. Initially, it might be painful to cut friendships with certain people. Some might get offended by your actions. But in the long run, it is for the betterment of all. We all have done this in one or the other way earlier, recognizing bad people and maintaining distance from them. However, this time I am requesting you to take a serious stand on it. You can't be playing with your opportunity of this life to please people for a while.

You need not change everything or everyone. Be concerned more about the five to ten people you spend most of your time with. If your core circle is strong, you need not worry about the rest. Moreover, it isn't about cutting your social circle. You may increase it, but at the same time, you shall learn to be more conscious about who you are letting in, what energy it is creating, and what qualities it is escorting in your life. Completely changing your company is not a viable option. After all, these people can be your parents, spouse, or best friends. In such a case, instead, learn not to embed their limited beliefs and relish your time with them.

Action Challenge: Write down two actions you need to take to improve your chances of living a successful life (financially, emotionally, and physically)

CHAPTER FOUR

LINE UP YOUR INTERNAL DRIVERS

It's a boon to be able to develop passion at an early age. However, those not so lucky should not get disheartened. The only way to find passion is by seeking one's vast array of interests. When you dare to try twenty different things, sooner or later you realize you have a passion for one of them. You learn to distinguish between being interested and being enthusiastic about something. You will notice, though you may be game for many things, you have the vehement burning desire only for certain things.

Most of us are waiting for our passion to land in our backyard. We think, one fine day, we will find our passion. We keep waiting for it as if it's going to walk in by itself. We barely take any actions to discover our passion. We don't know what action to take. I was also a part of the group that desperately waited to discover their passion. But then I realized this: I can't find my passion until I get my hands dirty, in say, twenty different things.

Ever since I started following successful people, I have been wondering what my passion could be. Today, I can finally say one of my passions is writing. How did I find out? By having the courage to try it. However, writing was not the only thing that I undertook. I also tried online business, trading, selling, consulting and valuing stocks with the same amount of encouragement. But that encouragement did not last long. I found myself bored easily. I felt those aren't something I can do for a lifetime. In the case of writing, it seemed so easy. Though it still needed me to do activities I don't cherish much like researching, collaborating, etc., yet it seemed easier than everything else in this world. There's a scientific term for this ease you experience while working on your passion. It's called "flow". It was coined by Mihaly Csikszentmihalyi, the author of Flow: The Psychology of Optimal Experience. It's a state of complete immersion in an activity. It's when something comes out of you without an effort.

I was not a born writer. Infact, I did not write even a single article before I wrote this book. Yet, when I started writing this book, it seemed so natural to me. Many times I wondered how am I able to express myself so beautifully? I couldn't understand whether it's just me who is expressing or the universe? 'Find your passion' is a common advice everyone has been giving for eons. The suggestion has such an enormous impact that a study conducted on United States teens found that people care more about having a job or career they enjoy than making a lot of money.[4.1] They are convinced passion is imperative because they have somewhere at the back of their mind, correlated passion with success and happiness. They have started to believe that they will be more successful and happier if they find and follow their passion.

All of us show an interest in more than one thing in our lifetime. Steve Jobs was also not an exception. He had an interest in design, calligraphy, electronics, Zen Buddhism, and many others. His life was a combination of his interests, and all these together has given him his success. But was Steve successful because he had an interest in these areas? After all, there would be many in this world having similar interests, yet only Steve could build brands like Apple and Pixar. One primary reason behind his success could be his skill of building great businesses, along with his desire and purpose to build great products. He never worked for money. Forbes's top 10 world's richest people list attests to it. While Bill Gates topped the list for a long time, Steve was never in it. The funny part is, today, Apple has the highest market capitalization and even in the past there was a prolonged period when Apple's market capitalization was higher than Microsoft's. There was a period when Steve Jobs denied compensation while working as the CEO of Apple. Of Course, he had Apple's shares but let's not forget that all CEOs deserve and mint much more. Steve's purpose for building great products, his passion for design, his erudite skills in building business, and his reality distortion field proved to be the reasons behind Apple's success. Ultimately, his purpose was the lighthouse, which helped navigate his ship of passion.

Passion and purpose complement each other. Passion acts as your driver of focus, while purpose gives you direction. You can be passionate about something, but you wouldn't know what to do with your passion until you know your purpose. Passion alone isn't enough to keep you on the success track. You need a purpose to stick on the track longer.

When we know the "why," we get more inclined towards the "what." It has a ripple effect on our performance. All of us take a shower to stay clean. If cleanliness weren't essential, the practice of taking a shower wouldn't have arisen. Every time we are told to do something, we ask 'why.' Even if you ask a little boy to study, he asks why? If you can't give him a good reason to do so, he wouldn't listen.

The mutual fund industry in India has recognized this and has come up with goal-based investing. They have specific plans for retirement and children's education to make their clients remain invested for a longer time horizon. They are retaining more customers by using the 'why' behind their customers' investment goals. Even the teams that undergo arduous training for the Olympics or World Championships are reminded repeatedly, embedding it deep in their minds, the purpose for which they are playing - their country, not for themselves. Similarly, in various aspects of life, we see that the act's purpose is more important than the act itself. It has been seen time and again that when a person does a job with a higher cause in mind, he performs arduously well, compared to when he plays for himself. The higher cause drives the person and makes him achieve extraordinary success. That's the sole reason why so many NGOs are running successfully. The workers barely earn any money compared to what they could have outside. Thousands of people happily come forward to volunteer for free. They do it because they have assigned a higher cause to it, in their mind. Their purpose boosts their passion.

Sadly today, there is a massive bunch of people who hate their job. A lot of us do not have a purpose to go back to work except to earn money. A lot of us do not have the privilege to take a break and start again. If you can't follow what you love, you must develop a love for what you are doing. Sometimes it is not practical to change jobs. Sometimes reality gets us caught. If that's the case with you, do not despise your situation. Instead, learn to look at it from a different perspective.

There's no place for love when there's no good that can be seen. Reasons could either be catalytic or non-catalytic. Good reasons would catalyze your love for a job, and bad reasons would kill your zeal for it. There could be both good and bad to what you go behind. But the more you cling to the good, the more you would start loving it and thereby see promising results. To see the good in what you do, you need to associate something good with it. For example, you may start to see how it could help society or how it could make someone's day. However, if the bad overshadows the good and it is going against your values and principles, it's better to change your path. But if it's you, who is overly pessimistic about what you do, it's time to shift your perspective. Start to acknowledge the little good things. Every day, practice to see one good thing your work could contribute to you and the people around you or the society on the whole. With small changes in your perspective, you can shift the reality. Every day, practice to inhale the good and exhale the bad. Once you change your why, your results will also change. Say you are in sales, and you do your job solely to earn commissions; you will find it hard to justify yourself for what you are doing. The increase in your earnings by hard sell would not give you the sense of accomplishment you seek. There will always be something in your mind that will pinch you while selling. Although you would be happy to earn the commissions, you wouldn't feel the satisfaction you could get by selling with a good cause. If that satisfaction is missing, you will gradually start disliking your work and eventually yourself!

Besides, when you start focusing on 'how my product can add value to my client' instead of 'how I can fill my pocket,' you will sell more. Stop falling into a pitfall of guilt for doing your work. Instead, try to see how much you are simplifying your client's lives by selling them a product or how easy their life is becoming through your services. When you start to think you are doing it to help your clients rather than help yourself, they will listen to you more. The words coming out of your mouth would change for the better because of your changed objective. You wouldn't be forceful, yet would end up making good sales. The same can be applied while leading a team. The more you will do it to help them get better, the more they will listen and follow. Still don't buy it? Let me ask you a question. Who would you like to listen to - the one who is benefitting you or the one who benefits from you?

Though purpose and passion are good for a start, to fire your life's rocket, layer it up with a clear vision. A person with a tenacious vision is unstoppable. The world that we are in now is given to us by legendary visionaries like Mahatma Gandhi, Isaac Newton, Nikola Tesla, Franklin Roosevelt, and Andrew Carnegie. They envisioned a future that ordinary people could never fathom. They made it a reality when ordinary people were busy making their livelihoods. To give up on their visions was never their option. To them, failure meant nothing more than a random event. Their vision was precise and was as concrete as tangible objects.

Elon Musk is one of the visionaries of the 21st century who always thought he would do something with space, the internet, and renewable energy during his childhood. Despite building his first video game at the age of twelve, he did not get into the gaming business as he knew it would be too small to make a difference. He rather chose the Internet era and created his first company, Zip2. He is one of his kind, who has the caliber to transform the internet, colonize mars, build the fastest electric car and revolutionize energy resources all at the same time. Making payment in seconds isn't a dream anymore. Electric cars are already a reality. Hopefully, living on Mars wouldn't look impossible by the end of the 21st century. After Paypal's success, Musk invested all his money in Tesla, SpaceX, and SolarCity. He did not doubt his vision, nor was he afraid to take the risk. He believed in his ideas and went all-in with everything he had. That's not all. He has invested in "The boring company," "Deep Minds," and "Neuralink," and has revealed plans for some of the most revolutionary future technologies of the 21st century. He didn't achieve it by fluke as luck may favor once, definitely not every time. He envisions, works, fails, rises again, and moves forward to build a much better future for mankind. His vision is his indestructible armor, which shields all his endeavors during setbacks.

Another radical visionary, Bill Gates, after his success with Microsoft, took the challenge to eradicate polio from all over the world. Today, none of the countries except Afghanistan, Pakistan, and Nigeria have a single polio case. His endeavors are beyond the imagination of ordinary people. Through the Bill and Melinda Gates Foundation, he is solving the problems relating to sanitation & hygiene. He has developed a technology that converts sewage into drinkable water in just minutes, solving the drinking water and waste disposal issues together. This is only one example of what a man's vision to solve society's dirtiest problem can do. His foundation is currently working on eighty-one different unconventional health problems, trying to continuously prevent and treat infectious diseases such as HIV, malaria, tuberculosis, pneumonia, and diarrhea worldwide.[4.2] With consistent efforts and help from organizations worldwide, his foundation has reduced the death of under-5 children from 10 million to 5 million p.a. and is aiming to cut it by half by the year 2030.[4.3] Do you think all that was easy for him? With his resources, yes, but with the dedication it takes, I guess no.

When you have a vision, have it strong. Often we go clueless about what we want. Asking the right questions on a regular basis is the way out when you are in such a fix. Here are some of the questions you can ask:

What kind of services the world needs today?;

What could bring a considerable difference in the next twenty years?;

How can I impact more people through my work?;

What kind of work can take mankind forward?;

What work in my interest area could bring a vast difference?;

What issues would I like to eliminate from this world?

Keep thinking, give it enough time, discuss it with people but don't get caught up by their views.

Mahatma Gandhi says, "It's not the man that makes the vision; it's the vision that makes the man." India gained its Independence after two hundred years of British Raj in 1947. It is one of the few countries in the world that got its Independence through the non-violence movement. The clear vision of one exemplary person, Mahatma Gandhi, brought together the masses to fight the seemingly impossible battle without an army. Initially, when the movement started, nobody believed in his vision. Many Indian leaders did not support him and chose to fight a separate battle. Yet Gandhiji did not lose his confidence. He knew what he was doing and stayed true to his thoughts.

Along with his followers, he conducted several fasts lasting between three to twenty one days and launched a civil disobedience movement and noncooperation movement. He influenced people to boycott foreign goods, for which he was put behind bars and was also subjected to punishments. Yet, he and his followers did not halt their struggle for Independence. This became possible because he made the people of India believe in his vision. He filled the hearts of millions of people with the desire for freedom. He could do it because he could visualize it. Through his determination, he gathered the masses, created pressure against the British government, and won the battle of Independence.

If a long term vision weighs heavy on you, have a short one that is easier to materialize. You may succeed or fail. Having it is crucial. Craft a vision, stand by it, and do whatever it takes to make it a reality.

During the early 1970s, China was merely an agrarian country with a vast population and poor living standards. But the rapid growth in the successive years led to China's emergence as a global superpower. Currently, China is the second-largest economy and is considered an upper-middle-income country by the World Bank. China's contribution to global trade, defense, industrialization, and external affairs, along with its vast investment in Advanced Technologies, has clarified the stand it would take in the coming decades. It wasn't long ago when it had zero investment in Artificial Intelligence. Still, today it is very close to transforming itself into an AI superpower surpassing the United States. China has come up with various plans and massive investments by the government, along with the leading AI-centric startups Baidu, Alibaba, and Tencent, to fulfill its vision by 2030. China's progress thus far is an exemplary precedent to prove the power of a superior vision.

China could achieve this feat by having fifty year and hundred year plans. Rarely any country works in that format. Most of the nations have a five-year, fifteen-year or a twenty five year plan. Very few leaders plan for their country's vision for a period longer than their lifetime.

Another country with a strong vision statement is the UAE. One of the reasons Venezuela slipped into hyperinflation was its over-dependence on oil resources. The UAE, being one of the largest exporters of oil, learned its lesson from Venezuela's hyperinflation and realized that it could also witness economic turmoil if the oil prices fall in the future due to the availability of alternative energy resources. In response to this realization, the UAE started diversifying its economy. There was a time when Dubai derived nearly half of its GDP from its oil resources. However, today it's no longer an oil-based economy. Oil constitutes hardly 1% of its current GDP. To reduce its over-dependence on oil, the country shifted its attention to tourism, trade, transport, and real estate. In 2019, Saudi Arabia also joined UAE's leap to open its economy for foreign tourists to reduce its dependence on oil and came up with the Saudi Vision 2030 plan to diversify its economy, despite its conservative culture.

If you have a voracious appetite to materialize your dreams and that appetite does not suppress unless you see to it, you won't mind the endeavor it'd require. Your surroundings, your time, your situations - none of it can meddle with your dedication. You'd simply do it whenever the opportunity presents itself. Moreover, you wouldn't wait for an opportunity as such, you will make one. Umberto Eco, an Italian novelist, was true to this in letter and spirit. During an interview, he was asked how he manages to pursue writing, teaching, and philosophical studies simultaneously. He said, "I have a secret. Did you know what will happen if you eliminate the empty spaces from the universe, eliminate the empty spaces in all the atoms? The universe will become as big as my fist. Similarly, we have a lot of empty spaces in our lives. I call them interstices. Say you are coming over to my place. You are in an elevator, and while you are coming up, I am waiting for you. This is an interstice, an empty space. I work in empty spaces. While waiting for your elevator to come up from the first to the third floor, I have already written an article!." Whenever Umberto got time, he scrawled on his notebook endlessly, nonchalant to his surroundings. I request you to take a leaf out of his book. I agree that his case is a bit extreme. However, if you have an unflinching desire, you will always figure out a way.

Imagine that there's an epic war ahead, and you have a scarce arsenal in hand. What would you do if conceding defeat is not your option? You would have to be a man of intellect rather than a man of action. Sometimes when you have an arduous goal, it is important to see things the other way round. When you are short of time to materialize your vision, instead of trying to find time for work in your routine, allocate all the time needed to fulfill your vision and fit in the rest accordingly. Don't try to apportion time to your work. Rather, take work as the epicenter of your day and see if you could fit in the rest. Eliminate unnecessary time burglars draining your energy, and you will find all the space in this world to materialize your vision.

Action Challenge: For next one week, set aside five minutes to meditate on the purpose of your life. Try to do it preferably as the first thing in the morning. Second preferable time would be before sleeping.

CHAPTER FIVE

BREAK YOUR OWN RECORD

Do you remember how much time it took you to learn to write a to z perfectly?

Probably a year.

What about learning to walk?

A year and a half.

Did speaking take any less?

Perhaps not.

How about singing?

Only if that was any easier.

Let's consider one final question.

How about living a happy life?

Oops, it turns out we are still learning.

If each activity since your childhood took you so much time, why do you wonder if other pursuits of life would go your way any easier? Don't you think we expect too much out of the self without putting in the required effort? Do you think if you work hard in all facets of life, as you did while learning to walk or write, you would still fail? Well, I agree there are exceptions who genuinely face difficulty in learning simple things, but what are the odds of you being one of them?

When Facebook laid its foundation stone, it barely had any captivating features that it has today. It started as a social networking website for Harvard in 2004. As it gained popularity over the campus, Zuckerberg strategically expanded it to various other colleges and schools. In 2006, he opened it for the general public. When he initially launched it, Facebook's mere objective was to connect people. It didn't have a wall (2004), groups (2004), photo sharing and tagging (2005), news feed (2006), developer's platform (2007), Facebook connect (2008), open graph APIs(2010), like button(2010) and many other features it has today. The company took one step at a time, kept working persistently, and came up with what we know today as Facebook.[5.1]

So is the case with Amazon. Jeff Bezos didn't start the company with a thought to establish an all-encompassing market over the Internet. While working as Vice President in D.E. Shaw, he was mesmerized by the World Wide Web and was eager to dip his hands into a system growing at 2400% a year. He soon realized he needed to come up with a business idea to make the most of the upcoming revolutionary boom, and he could not think of anything better than Books. His idea was to build an online store providing the most significant book collection. He further started expanding his business into the field of music and videos. While pondering what else he could sell over the web, he surveyed a thousand randomly selected customers asking what else they would like to buy from Amazon? To his surprise, customers came up with all sorts of ideas. They mostly replied with the product names they were looking to buy at that very moment. Jeff was astonished by the replies and thought, "we can sell anything this way," and that's how the concept of "the everything store" was born.

Everything starts with a simple idea, and with every step of effort, it starts to become a reality. A few months back from writing this chapter, I could not even think of writing a paragraph myself. I convinced my cousin to write for me as writing is his forte. The plan was simple, I would give him ideas, and he would articulate it. Our partnership stood firm initially, but as he was also running a full-time business, he started to lose interest day by day. He stopped picking my calls for a month. However, I was determined to complete this book. I thought he would soon find the time, but it was all in vain. I spent days waiting for him to change his mind when suddenly one of my friends said, "Why don't you write it yourself. At least give it a try". For starters, I ignored his idea, being massively under-confident of my writing skills. Still, one night while I was lying down in my bed, a thought crossed my mind, and like lightning, I sat, opened my laptop, and started writing. I consistently wrote for ninety minutes every day for three months and later took it as a full-time job. Initially, every time I wrote, I was afraid of what and how I would write, but nonetheless I kept writing. I didn't give it a second thought and stayed unwavering on my journey.

Nothing worthwhile gets constructed in a day. Everything takes consistent and deliberate effort. So choose the thing you want to focus on, stay persistent, move forward one step at a time, and keep challenging yourself. Your biggest competition is the man in the mirror.

Ernest Hemingway has rightly said, "There is nothing noble in being superior to your fellow man; true nobility is in being superior to your former self." Life isn't a battle royale where you have to be better than everyone else. Plus, always beating everyone else gets boring pretty soon. You are your worthiest opponent, one who can evolve with you and can challenge you every day.

To challenge yourself each day, take-up activity in the area you want to improve and break your previous record by performing a little better each day. Make a note of the new baseline. Keep tracking your performance. Do not take up more than one activity. At a time, track one action for the most relevant activity that needs your attention.

For effective tracking, use an A4 sheet, divide it into seven rows and three columns. Write down the dates for the next twenty-one days in each part and use it to track the actions on the challenge you have taken up. Every day push your previous day's achievements and keep pushing it until you reach a saturation point; until your highest record becomes your new normal. Once you have exerted yourself enough in a specific direction, take up a different challenge, and repeat the process.

To start tracking your habit, refer to Part 2 - "21 Days of change" of the workbook.

Tracking is requisite because you wouldn't know if you are performing in your full capacity until you keep track. Instead of ending up with the perception that you did well, which may not be correct, get the facts right. It will give you a good reality check and will give you a baseline to cross every day. It's essential to track your actions on a single sheet of paper to aid comparison. A handy comparison boosts performance. It works as a source of motivation. Moreover, it's much easier to carry a piece of paper all the time in your bag to jot down things whenever necessary. If you have a list of things to write, use a diary. But make sure it's handy and doesn't require any extra effort to pen down your notings.

Here are some of the rules for successful tracking:

1. Do not track your goals. Track your actions.

2. Track measurable actions like miles you run, hours you work, calories you intake, questions you solve, number of pages you read, clients you meet, etc.

3. Have integrity while tracking. Be honest with the sheet of paper. Assume it's watching you.

4. Don't track everything. It will become overwhelming, and you will give up too soon.

While you track your performance, push yourself one step at a time. If you want to improve your health, stretch your yoga timings by five minutes every day. If you are studying for exams, solve two extra questions. If you want to acquire a new skill, spend five extra minutes each day than your previous day. The simpler the tracker, the easier it is to follow.

Success is nothing but an accumulation of small right habits. These habits, when followed religiously for an extended period, deliver astounding results. The results may take time, but when you measure yourself by your daily successes, you stay on track and save yourself from negative feelings of failure. Success and failure aren't definite, but good outcomes are always possible when you are constantly moving ahead in the right direction. When you challenge yourself and grow every day, the outcome can't be wrong. Results may take time, but they would eventually come your way.

Wherever you are today, there is a scope for improvement. But, sometimes in life, as we reach a point of comfortable growth and achievement, we become stagnant. It mostly happens after we have created a fine amount of wealth and relations, have got enough favorable outcomes from our endeavors, and have got most of what we have always desired. In such a circumstance, many settle down with it. They forget what else they can create, what extra capabilities they have, how much better they can be. It's called reaching a comfort zone from where any step further looks a bit unnecessary and undesirable.

It's like saying I want to keep my money in a savings account because I have already created a fair amount of wealth. You forget that your biggest enemy, inflation, is still alive. Keeping money in a savings account and letting it grow at a lesser interest rate than inflation is like saving money only to see it less valuable in the future. It isn't that an unusual mistake. People do it often. Because they have generated a good income source, they take their success for granted and think that their fate would always favor them. They forget that the only thing that's predictable about the future is its unpredictability.

Likewise, we make similar mistakes in our personal and professional life. We start taking things for granted and forget that one day our fate can outwit us, whether in the form of competition or the loss of someone. Sometimes, we forget that our desire was indeed much bigger than what we have achieved, but since we have a fair share of it, we try to settle down and excuse ourselves from the hard work. This problem isn't confined to success. It has its root in case of constant failures despite improvements. We become stagnant when we know we deserve it but can't see things moving favorable. If you think you are standing near this zone, you need to shift your outlook. You need to see that growth is the only constant you can have, whether positive or negative. As I am writing this chapter, today it's been sixteen months since the first covid-19 case was found in India. The world has seen various lockdowns. The way businesses operate has been completely transformed. But, did you even feel for a second that everything would collapse? No. Not at all. Despite listening to news channels who do a great job in spreading negativity, Earth hasn't lost its hope. We know from our heart that we will recover from this loss.

To remind yourself of your abilities, refer to Part 3 - "Be your hero" of the workbook.

Don't get disheartened with the ups and downs of life. There was not one time when today's most successful businesses were on the cliff of failure. They had their share of bad luck through recessions, wars, competition, regulations, poor management, etc. yet, nothing stopped them from being what they are today.

Elon Musk's Tesla was on the verge of bankruptcy in 2013 with a week's cash remaining. The acquisition deal by Google was the only viable option. However, meanwhile the discussions with Larry Page, Musk gave it one last chance by asking all five hundred employees of his company to leave everything they were doing and get into selling. If those employees had not sold huge volumes of cars in a few weeks, Tesla would not have announced their first profit in 2013 and would have become part of Alphabet Inc.[5.2] That wasn't once when his company tumbled, nor is he alone whose company faced cash crunching.

In the 1860's US presidential election, Abraham Lincoln won the presidency by a mere 39.8% of votes, which says there were 60.2% of people who stood against him. In the 2016 US presidential election, Donald Trump was outwitted by Hilary Clinton by 2% of votes, yet he won it. There were more than 50% of people who didn't believe in Trump. Whether you have someone who believes in you, you must believe in yourself. Don't doubt your capabilities even when people are dead sure of your failure. People like to predict, and they have fun doing that. Don't limit yourself because others think you can't do it. Take up new challenges and reward a better version of yourself each day.

Action Challenge: Write down an area you are playing small despite your interest. Track it for the next twenty-one days and enjoy your new self.

CHAPTER SIX

STOP FOOLING YOURSELF

An average person lies at least once a day. But the lies that he tells himself are uncountable. Most people have a good heart and always want to do the right thing. They try to be truthful in their dialogue. Yet they aren't very honest to themselves.

"I'll hit the gym tomorrow."

"Only if I had enough time, I would've cracked the exams."

"I did what I could."

"I don't have much time; I'll do it later."

The last one is the most destructive because it feeds upon itself, pulling us down into an unproductive abyss. That's not all. We also lie in attributing our reasons for failure to reasons like lack of motivation, lack of resources, lack of guidance, lack of luck, lack of nepotism, lack of this, and lack of that. We actually lack a lot in being truthful to ourselves.

You may have found yourself uttering words in the league of "I'm too old/young/poor/busy," "I am not Bill Gates/Elon Musk/God," "I don't have the right connections/skills for this job." Let us today accept all our lies. Let us stop attributing our failures to anything/anyone. Let's admit, most of the time, we did not move our butt to get what we wanted.

Stop fooling yourself by thinking you are tired, hungry, unmotivated, or unskilled when you are plain lazy. Learn to differentiate when you are tired and when you are outright making up excuses. Address both of the situations differently. When you are tired, take a rest; when you are distracted, take a deep breath.

Every time you say to yourself, 'I CAN'T,' breathe deeply for a few seconds, sit calm and think again, 'CAN I'? If yes, then start working. At least give it a try. It's okay if the answer is no. Maybe your schedule doesn't permit it, you have a different priority, you don't have money, or it doesn't align with your values. If you have realized 'YOU CAN,' but the work seems like a big deal, start with one step at a time; divide the task; figure out how you can turn it into reality, whose help you might need, and what actions you need to take. Within no time, you will realize things have started to move.

Meditate on your feelings, mood, and ideas that shape your mind, rather than arriving at nugatory conclusions. Right from rolling out of bed till you hit the sack, there's always a person inside you from the subconscious world trying to strike a conversation with your conscious mind. Often one pays little heed to it. For a change, listen to the inner chatter diligently. Stay ahead in catching yourself by being aware of the real reason hidden in your mind. We make the mistake of never listening to what's going on inside and try to change everything happening outside.

Develop the discipline to walk the talk. Do what you say. It should be basic and not an addition. In the military, discipline is indispensable. If the military had not established protocols and training, soldiers would not be able to take right actions in extreme conditions. Their arduous gut-wrenching curriculum has developed them into warriors who, instead of getting stressed in a dreadful condition, strike back within seconds. They are mentally and physically trained for outrageous conditions. And if they can fight back in those moments you can surely train yourself for everyday challenges.

Discipline requires robust willpower. For a long time, researchers thought that willpower is dependent on the glucose level. Having a sugary drink was the prescription for it. However, the latest research has found that willpower has got nothing to do with glucose level. Of course, eating healthy and maintaining a general glucose level is vital for the body's healthy functioning, willpower doesn't require an injection of sugar.

To conduct the research, Veronika Jobs gave one group of people an easy task and another group of people a challenging task, followed by a cognitive task. The cognitive task required self-control to avoid mistakes. Results showed that people who believed willpower is limited made twice the mistake on cognitive tasks. Those who believed willpower is unlimited, performed well on challenging tasks irrespective of what their first task was. [6.1]

If one believes he has willpower, he exerts more of it. Isn't that easy? You have to think you have more of it, and you have it. Use this new resource of willpower to develop the discipline in your life. Do not force yourself to be disciplined in everything you do. Find the areas that need it, like studying for 3 hours a day, spending an hour to hone your skills, or hitting the gym. Do not worry about not being disciplined in cleaning your bed. That hardly matters. Though it does help to build your mental muscles by fighting your mood and emotions, it won't give its service in making you successful.

Train your mind to evolve yourself into a person who says it and does it. But choose what you say wisely because otherwise, you will have to jump into anything and everything. Learn to judge yourself like a third person objectively. Once you become your judge, you may fool others but not yourself. Stand true to your words. Once you commit, do not look back. Don't let your laziness, hesitation, and under-confidence topple you down. If you have decided to do something, do it without fail.

In 1972, Dr. Phil A. Silva started the arduous Dunedin study on 1037 children born within a year in Queen Mary Maternity Hospital. He studied children's physical and psychological behavior in childhood. He continued to assess them in an interval of two to six years throughout their lives. Today, 916 participants are still a part of this study. They are invited to Dunedin city at every assessment, where they go through a series of interviews, physical tests, questionnaires and surveys examining their health, wealth, and crime involvement.

The study helped to surface one of the most surprising truths about human behavior. It revealed that childhood self-control has more influence over adult success than IQ and social status. The children who had higher self-control in childhood later showed lower criminal convictions, lower health issues, and higher financial success. While those who had lower self control in infancy showed more health and money related issues. For years we thought that IQ and family background contribute to adult success. However, the Dunedin study found that self-control is a stronger predictor for success than what is generally believed.

Develop self-control to manage your emotions and temptations. Stop giving attention to your thoughts like "I am bored," "I don't feel like doing it now," "I hate doing that stuff," etc. The more you talk and think about it, the heavier that emotion becomes. Stop thinking, forget that feeling, and get engaged. It's just a thought, and it would go away once you allow something else in your mind. Once you jump into the work, your mind will throw you new ideas to think upon, and you will forget the negative feelings you had for your work.

In general, all of us stick to our plan, but in our heads, we know we are avoiding some part of it because we are afraid to do it.

We keep working on the easy stuff and keep postponing the real work that needs to be done. We fool ourselves by making us believe we are working hard and ditch the challenging part to save ourselves from the strenuous process.

While I was writing this book, I had this quote stuck in my wall by Eleanor Roosevelt: "Do one thing every day that scares you." Though I was working in my full capacity, this quote kept reminding me of the work I was running from. Every time I read it, I felt a twinge in my stomach. It evoked in me the sudden need to do the work I was avoiding and made me bring to my consciousness my internal reluctance for scary work. For a writer, writing is easy, but activities like applying to publishers, reframing the book to make it reader-centric, or research doesn't feel soothing. And at different points in time, I was reluctant to do these because they looked scary. That's the trigger point. If something looks dangerous, that's exactly what you have to do. That's the work that can take you closer to your goals faster. Make it a point to do the thing that scares you every day. Ask yourself, "what am I running from?". Your fear is the answer. Work on what you fear the most.

A great way to trick yourself into serious action is by picking a role model. Being absorbed in the person you want to become, could introduce changes in you without your notice. Say you want to be the person who has excessive knowledge, you may think of Elon Musk or Hermione Granger from Harry Potter, the girl who happens to know everything. Imagine yourself becoming a bibliophile like them. Follow their footsteps of reading thousands of books and experimenting with encyclopedic knowledge.

A study conducted by Dumas and Dunbar found that the way we instantiate creativity stereotypes can have different effects. Depending on the character's choice, a character's personification may increase or decrease one's creativity. The study shows that a person exhibit superior creative performance when he tries to solve a creative problem by imagining himself as an eccentric poet than as a rigid librarian.[6.2] By imagining yourself as a poet, i.e., an uninhibited personality type, you can tap into your creative persona. While trying the opposite, do not expect to mesmerize your audience. You can perform superiorly well by shifting your outlook. If you want to thrive in business, you may think of yourself as a super successful businessman who is always on his toes. It is one such way to invariantly transform yourself into a doer from being just a complacent bummer.

Another way to make the action easier in life is through practicing visualization. Most of us spend time imagining ourselves living our dream life. But we forget to imagine the arduous work our goal needs. We see ourselves living in a beautiful mansion, driving the costliest car, having a lavish vacation, or running a multinational corporation. But never do we focus our mind on imagining the hard work it requires.

The research was conducted on the modulation of muscle response by dividing people into two groups. One group played a simple sequence of piano notes. In contrast, the other group imagined playing the same sequence for five consecutive days. Both groups got their brains scanned each day. The results were astonishing. The group that played the piano and the group that visualized playing the piano had similar brain changes.[6.3]

Another experiment was conducted by psychologist Alan Richardson. He divided the subjects into three groups. Group A was asked to practice free throws of basketball for twenty minutes, five days a week. Group B was asked to not even think about basketball. Group C was asked to visualize free throws under an instructor for twenty minutes, five days a week. The experiment continued for four weeks. The results showed that Group A, who actually performed the task improved their free throws by twenty-four percent. Group B did not improve as expected. However, Group C which did not do anything except practicing visualization, improved by twenty-three percent, one percent lesser than Group A.

Visualization has been a very common practice among sports players. Nineteen-year-old Bianca Andreescu who won over Serena Williams in US Open final shares that she had been practicing visualization since she was twelve. Every single day, she visualized how she would tackle different situations on the court. This is just one example. There are many others.

Let's say you are a salesman, and you are looking to make big commissions. No matter how much you love to earn money, deep down you hate the strenuous work it takes. The traditional method to achieve goals emphasizes imagining your bank account getting credited with hefty commissions. But working on our brain isn't that simple. When we imagine the end result, our mind starts to believe that we have already achieved them. As we saw above, our brain isn't capable of distinguishing between imagination and reality. It responds to both in similar ways. It enjoys the emotion and feeling created by the imaginative process. It believes the result has already been accomplished when, in reality, you are far away from your goals. This way, the brain gets the privilege of enjoying the results without actually achieving it.

That doesn't mean we shouldn't be thinking of the result. Imagination is great, but we must be conscious of our imagination process and not get lost, perceiving it as reality. It's tough but not impossible. As Napoleon Hill said, "whatever the mind of a man can conceive and believe, it can achieve." We should picturize our dreams to devise it in our minds. Creating the belief is an integral part of the journey. However, to complete the journey, it is crucial to imagine the process of actual work that needs to be done. When we do that, we get accustomed to the task. If you are a salesman, the various options to imagine can be your interactions with the client, your requests for referrals, sales presentation, or conversations while closing deals. This visualization process eases the actual effort. When you practice these scenarios in your head, you do not feel exhausted when you actually do it, even if you dislike it. You would think of it as a part of your routine and wouldn't consider it strange and out of the box.

Winner of the gold medal in the 400m hurdle in the 1992 Olympics, Sally Gunnell attributes 70% of her winning to visualization. She says after coming second at the 1991 World Championships, she visualized herself running fast, crossing every hurdle, and even dealing with the exhaustion at the end of the race over and over again. She says this process helped her win the gold by toughening her muscles even when she was not practicing.

The practice of imagining the process well prepares our brain for the physical and mental exhaustion we would be going through. It prepares us for the obstacles we will be facing and the discomfort we will be having while making that challenging move. Alex Honnold, famously known for his free solo climbing on El Capitan, says he visualized climbing the mountain for 48 hours before his climbing day. He imagined every move he would be making, everything that could happen, and every handhold and foothold he would be using. That's the preparation he did before his climb. Every climber uses ropes and safety gear, but Alex used none of it.

Alex did not visualize himself enjoying the joyous moment after the work, nor did Sally imagine herself winning the gold. Doing that would have been very soothing and fun. But they knew that would not help in making their dream a reality. Winning does not require envisioning the things that come after. It requires you to envision the hard moves you would be making. It requires you to visualize every step with crystal clarity, every obstacle you would have to overcome, and the effort it would need.

The more we focus on the result, the slower our progress would be. The more we focus on the path, the quicker we get to our destination. So do not fool your brain by letting it imagine what's not real. Instead, prepare it for the real work by visualizing the process. Do what is required, don't get caught up by your mood, stand objectively for your goals, and be true to yourself. Look closely into your behavior and judge yourself like a third person. Take better daily actions and decisions. Only then can you not fool yourself.

Action Challenge: Pick an area you want to improve. Find a role model. Immerse their qualities into yourself and act like them.

CHAPTER SEVEN

WHEN CELLS ARE IN HARMONY

Our bodies can not function successfully without harmony among our cells. When a single cell out of the blue starts working against the other cells, it triggers diseases like cancer and autoimmune disorders. These diseases are merely a response to misfunctioning among cells. When our cells start multiplying uncontrollably, it causes cancer. When they attack other healthy cells, it gives birth to diseases like thyroid, arthritis, and vitiligo.

Dr. Bruce Lipton says, "there is not one function in the human body that is not already present in every single cell." From systems like digestion, respiration, reproduction to having an individual nervous system, and immune system, all the functions exist in each cell of our body. We are nothing but an accumulation of cells. When these cells work in harmony, our body functions appropriately. When they do not, diseases occur. As our cells need harmony for proper body functioning, our goals need harmony among our thoughts. When we move single-mindedly towards a goal, accomplishing it becomes much more comfortable. A challenging goal requires collective power. Like a single person can't push an SUV, while a group of men can; we can't accomplish our goals half-mindedly

There's a lovely term in Chinese called "Wu Wei." It means "non-doing" or "effortless doing." It's a state of mind that gets things done effortlessly. As per followers of Taoism, one can only do effortless doing when he is at ease, is completely aware, and is in alignment with the natural cycles of the world. You must have noticed, many times it takes you twice the time to complete a task simply because you weren't present to it wholeheartedly. Thoughts kept crossing your mind, ideas kept evoking in your head, making it harder and harder to focus. A small insect, a coworker's noise, or a popup on a webpage is enough to disturb our harmony and makes us feel tired without getting anything done.

When our body and environment are in harmony, our performance improves significantly. We all are well aware of this fact, then why do we allow distractions? Why do we let it happen? Why don't we take action to stop it? One primary reason being, we rarely experience work without distraction. We are so prone to distraction that we have forgotten there can be an alternative. We have forgotten that we can provide ourselves the liberty to work in isolation. We have the power. We have the choice but we forget to access it. Working in a distracting environment has become so common that we have forgotten the alternative is available. If complete isolation is not possible, try to set aside at least three hours of isolated distraction-free work time.

Sadly, the distraction is not always external. A lot of it happens internally as well. Some of us have an exceptional habit of fantasizing about a thought. I know people who have spent hours daydreaming. How do I know? I was one of them. Daydreaming is a vicious cycle. Victims of it know that the inner chattering and imagination is a never-ending journey. Some enjoy worrying as much as ice cream. They have developed a habit of it. They worry about what they would eat for dinner, what they would wear for an upcoming party, when they would prepare their presentation, what people would think of them, and the list goes on. It does not help them except for increasing their cortisol levels.

Instead of worrying, learn to be intentional and appreciative of the activity you are doing. Develop the habit of being present at the moment, and you will find yourself much happier and productive. If you are working, try not to drift off into daydreams. Thinking about what's for dinner or the weather isn't helping you get your work done any better.

Being completely present in the moment does not only apply to your work. It applies equally while spending time with your family. Give them your full attention. Your kids and significant others would be happy to find you not worrying about the upcoming deadline. Even if you can provide only thirty minutes to your partner, be sure to give them your complete attention. Every living organism seeks attention, and so does your wife, kids, dog, friends, and colleagues. They will appreciate it and understand the next time you'll need some extra time to complete an important project or need some alone time.

I have personally taken this concept very seriously. I hardly use my cellphone when people are around. I prefer to sit in isolation from the crowd, even in a restaurant. I sit facing towards the wall to avoid getting distracted from any movement that might happen in front. I write and shoot late at night when everyone is asleep. While spending time with family, none of us are allowed to use phones. When I meet someone, I prefer to adjust my chair facing the person while ensuring that nothing is visible behind them. These small habits have become a part of me. I don't put effort into doing it. I do it out of habit. When small choices get followed consciously, they develop as habits and bring massive differences in our being.

When I was a child, there came a phase in my schooling, where I believed that none of the students in the class could get more than 95% in a subject. I thought teachers would cut marks somewhere or the other, probably because someone in my family randomly said so (another impact of the subconscious). I felt it's a waste of time for me to even try to attain that, and that's when I began to aim for less because I thought it wasn't possible. This pattern continued until, to my surprise, I got 98 marks in maths in 8th Grade! That was the moment my misbelief vanished. I realized it's possible, and all those years, I had been fooling myself despite being a class topper.

In various instances of life, we do not try because in our head we have decided that it's not possible. Many of us do not even try to talk to our boss about a promotion. We do not try to step towards financial freedom. After a certain age, many of us stop trying to learn new things. Rarely do we try to mold our relations with our loved ones. We carry wrong beliefs and stop ourselves from giving it one full try.

Fear of failure also catches us. The fear isn't real. We make it up in our subconscious. We fail the situation in our minds so miserably that we think it's not even worth a try. We behave as if we will be put behind bars if we fail. Sadly, society does give us that feeling at times. But more than the community, we are the ones responsible for our miserable feelings. We carry the feeling of failure so close to our heart that even if people around us aren't aware of our past failures, deep inside, we feel miserable around them.

This reminds me of another funny story from my childhood. When I was in Grade II, we had a science class test, and my best friend got nineteen out of twenty. She asked me about my marks, but I was so devastated and ashamed of my performance that even though she continuously asked for it, I replied nothing. Wondering what my marks were? I got seventeen in that test. Seventeen! Not ten, not five, not two. Just two marks less than my best friend. Now when I look back, I laugh at myself. But you seem to miss the feeling of shame that small girl carried in her heart that day. The shame was created by her and not by the people around her. It was on her mind! Nobody would have said anything to her for getting two marks lesser than her best friend. Nobody would have even cared about her marks. Yet the pain was so deep that I remember it even today. Understand the degree to which we are getting affected by our fallacies. Our situations look entirely different when we reflect on them after a few years. Most of us laugh, recollecting the memories. However, no one can recoup the suffering it created then. It wasn't obligatory. We created it. And so we have the power to destroy it. We have to make sure that it does not affect us, not outwit us. We need to see that we do not fall for pity issues. We need to pause the hallucination from stopping ourselves in our journey. We have to make conscious attempt to make use of our full potential.

Since we were born, we have been carrying the baggage of the past, stepping into the future and in between forgetting our present. The past is history; the future is an illusion, while the present is the truth. Be more grateful for the present. The classic idea of meditation runs on the backbone of consciousness. All the meditation courses are teaching us to be in the "now". There surely must be some good reason behind it! Being in now does not just make you productive. It helps you remove negativity, fight stress, focus on action rather than thinking, and in the end, make you happy and peaceful.

Instead of only being present, I request you to take it to another level and apply this rule in every aspect of your life. Make yourself 100% accountable. Have 100% faith in yourself. Start taking 100% responsibility for your life, your relationships, your successes, and your failures. There's no good in playing the blame game. In the end, the world would be a better place if we all took 100% responsibility for ourselves.

When my friend Revanth Narava told me, he cleared an exam with an All India Rank(AIR) 1, I was intrigued. Knowing his past achievements of passing all the Chartered Accountancy levels with an AIR, I wasn't surprised much. Still, the thought of how he does it every time kept ringing bells in my head. I finally decided to ask him his secret, and here's the answer I got, he said: "I decide it, and I do it." He shared he runs his life by the mantra of "getting it done at any cost." He doesn't know any other way of living life. He gets the similar obstacles we all get. He clears it off like we all do but never does he fall short on what he sets as his goal. Throughout his childhood, he was always a class topper. He never secured less than Rank 3 in his life. Today, even in his office, he is well recognized for his work among his seniors. This guy proves that success is a habit. He built on this habit in his early childhood by identifying the positive reaction he got from society. He realized, people like him more because of his achievements. That was one of his initial motivations, which soon capitalized on the idea of achieving targets in any case.

When he decided to prepare for the exam while working full time, he bifurcated the left days into two parts. Months required him to perform at his best in the office, say year-end in case of audits and months when there was low work pressure. By dividing his time, he neither had to compromise on his profession nor in his studies. He successfully gave his 100% in both the arenas. He studied in lunch breaks during his office hours, compromised on parties, did not waste time on Netflix but still managed to have a good time with his girlfriend and family members.

You may find this advice of giving your 100% clichéd, but how many times in a day do you think you operate with 100% of your capacity? What difference do you think it can make if you operate with your complete self all the time? What variations can this way of living bring into your life? Try it for a day, if not a year, and see the difference. When you are sure of its benefits, develop it as a habit.

Another significant factor required to bring harmony in your actions is to have well-defined core values. When I started selling investment products, I majorly had two products on my hand- investment plans by insurance companies and mutual funds. Having vast knowledge of finance, I was well aware that most of my clients' portfolios need mutual funds instead of endowment plans. In case you don't know, upfront commissions paid by insurance companies for endowment plans are twenty times higher than those paid by mutual fund companies. Also, insurance companies keep running attractive contests every month to motivate their partners. By attractive, I mean anything that ranges between the price of a laptop to a short free foreign trip. That's one reason you find numerous people doing whatever it takes to sell you insurance products, while in the case of mutual funds, agents are much at ease. After selling a few products, I knew I could not give the advice that I should have been giving.

I was selling good, safe, profitable products, but they weren't in my clients' best interest. Though I was earning well, my conscience was not satisfied. I realized that my deeds were not aligned with my values. As the agitation continued, I became more certain about the significance I had been carrying in my mind of giving the right advice to my clients. One of the core values I live by is "doing the right thing." Though I did go off track for some time, my core values made me conscious of my mistake and brought me back on track. I decided to stop being pushy and promised myself not to run behind attractive contests.

But then I had another dilemma. Since I performed well in a short time, I was very close to winning an ongoing contest, which would have given me a chance to win a free foreign trip apart from commissions and other incentives. I wondered if I should continue selling insurance merely for a month to win this trip. I knew it wouldn't take me much effort. But then what about my core values?

I decided to discuss it with a trusted friend. I explained the situation and clarified that I earned eighty percent of my income by selling insurance last month, and I am close to winning a free foreign trip. His reply was brisk and straightforward. He said, "what you can't do forever shouldn't be done at all." I got my answer. The conversation ended there itself. And that very moment, I decided that I won't advise insurance plans until my client genuinely needs it. And I have not sold even a single insurance product till date.

Well defined written core values are best to have. They make your decision making simpler and bring harmony between your actions and thoughts. It stops the friction inside your body and connects you towards your higher calling. Here are some examples of core values to live by:
- honesty
- altruism
- excellence
- perfectionism
- authenticity
- being helpful
- being loving and kind
- righteousness
- integrity
- valuing customers
- humbleness
- mastery
- innovation

Core values can't be fostered in a day. It requires constant contemplation and some robust experiences. Various situations in life teach you lessons that mold your values. The lessons learned shall not be forgotten as most of the time, they guide you more than your successes.

Core values are highly subjective, and hence only via personal experience, a person can define them. You can never live by other values. You can only find your own. The easiest way to define them is to look into the feelings and the emotions that guide you into everyday action. If introspection makes you restless deep inside, it's highly probable that you have derailed. In such a situation, ask yourself- Did I do justice to what I did? If the answer is no, it's time to acknowledge the values you already have.

Start being attentive to the constant arguments you have in your head. Contemplate your thoughts and watch out for your actions that have hurt you the most in the past. Make a list of your past activities that pinch you every time you think of them. Some event that doesn't make you feel at ease. That's where you might not have stood by your values. Write them down. Think for a while, why does it make you feel bad? What wrong did you do? Don't look for activities that hurt you because someone else did something to you. Look for areas where people were neutral, but you felt bad for your actions. That's the place your values are hidden. Spend a few days thinking about it.

To formulate your core values, refer to Part 4 - "Living by the values" of the workbook.

According to Deloitte, organizations driven by a mission have a thirty percent higher innovation level and forty percent higher employee engagement.[7.1] Starbucks is one company that was clear about its values from the beginning. That's one reason why Howard Schultz decided to work with Starbucks and later bought it from its founders. He admired the company's values and decided to build it further into a brand that exists for its quality, employee, customers, and ethical practices. That's one reason why it has a low employee turnover ratio, excellent customer service, and a heartwarming environment. In the era where cost-cutting was the norm, Starbucks created health care plans for its employees, working as little as twenty hours a week. It calls its employees' partners' and offers stock options to its employees proportionate to their pay scale. That's not all. When Howard Schultz realised that the number one benefit Chinese employees want is a health care plan for their parents, he accepted it. At that time, there was not even a single company that offered this benefit.

Starbucks never compromised its quality and values for higher profits. It proudly owns the badge of Fortune World's Most Admired Companies and World's Most Ethical Companies.[7.2] That became possible because Starbucks had a clear mission statement. They knew what they wanted, and they adhered to it.

Action Challenge:

Write down two areas where you are playing below standard? Write down one action you would take to level up your game.

CHAPTER EIGHT

WHY DO WE PROCRASTINATE AND WHAT TO DO ABOUT IT?

Ask a hundred people regarding their procrastination habit, and they would say it has been the most persistent! Their favorite hobby has also not stayed consistent as much as their habit of procrastination. We all love to procrastinate. We rarely find anyone saying he likes to do the work as it comes. And if one does that, it would be too foolish!

Procrastination is a good choice. Had it not been, we could never have worked flawlessly. Because we procrastinate, we can focus on the ongoing task. If we were to do everything as it comes, I doubt the quality we would have produced. However, prolonged procrastination isn't good either.

Studies show a positive correlation between stress, lack of self-compassion, and procrastination. When someone lacks self compassion, they criticize and blame themselves for petty reasons. When repeated, this behavior boosts negative emotions. It gives them good reasons to put things off repeatedly which further gives rise to stress.[8.1]

Dr. Tim Pychyl, professor of psychology, says, "Procrastination is an emotion regulation problem, not a time management problem."[8.2] Most of us think we cannot check off our complete list because we are bad at time management. That does have some truth in terms of scheduling. Still, mostly, it's the emotions we are into at the moment that formulates our responses. When we feel confident, we happily take up a challenging task, but feeding the birds also seems irritating when we are feeling low.

You must have noticed, every time you approach a work, a series of dialogues starts in your head. Our mind has so much to speak to us all the time. It never stops with its reasons. It can argue over anything using its fallacies. Some of the typical dialogues crossing your head must be:

"I don't feel like doing it";

"I have done enough work today";

"It's neither urgent nor important";

"I have more important work to be done."

However, the real meaning could be somewhere in the lines of:

"I find it boring";

"The work is too strenuous";

"It's too hard";

"I hate it."

Try digging a layer further inside your inner dialogues, and you will find another range of reasons you are unaware of. They can be anything related to:

"I am not good enough,"

"I am too afraid to do it,"

"I am surely going to fail," etc.

You can feel the presence of this third layer of dialogue while postponing critical tasks. The upper layer of dialogues is superficial, while the end layer showcases the real reason behind your procrastination. Emotions are a colossal driver behind our decisions. When they are negative, they restrain you. When they are positive, they help you.

Dialogues are a continuous part of your mind. You may not have noticed yet these have acted as a driving force in your decisions. They acted in the background, in your subconscious. The only way to get rid of them is by being more aware of them and paying attention to them. Get a hold over the real reasons by giving enough attention to the voice in your head. Being mindful is the only way to consciously argue with your inner self and convince yourself to take the right actions.

Next time when you find yourself procrastinating, list down five to ten possible reasons. Don't focus on writing the superficial ones. Dig a little deeper. Find the second and third layers of the reason for the ones you have listed. Do it till you reach a point where you are completely convinced by your answer. Keep practicing this technique until it becomes natural for you to figure out the real reasons behind your procrastination. As you will learn to interrogate yourself on different occasions, you will also get a knack for solving other problems. Moreover, you will realize, most of the time, you did not have a good reason to postpone something, but you did it out of habit.

Yes, procrastination is a habit. The more we are practicing it, the stronger it becomes. With the number of times we have procrastinated, it has become part of a routine. This habit, like every other habit, rewards us. The first and biggest reward we get is the relief of not doing the work. Most of the time, we procrastinate mindlessly without even thinking for a second. We are always in search of immediate gratification. Whatever makes us happy is welcome at any hour of the day. By procrastinating, we reward ourselves by eliminating the effort. And who doesn't get pleased with the reduction of work? This reward is so close to our heart that we ignore the cost involved. From skipping yoga sessions to going shopping when we should be working, a large part of the reason can be attributed to our thirst for immediate rewards.

Another psychological reason behind procrastination is that we never think of the latest work as part of our routine. We procrastinate long before we are supposed to do it because we see it as an additional work on top of our workload. To not postpone the critical jobs, learn to incorporate them into your routine by assigning them a specific space and time. Block off some time in your routine even for tasks that require as little as fifteen minutes. Make yourself sit with the right tools, and within no time, you would find yourself genuinely engaged in it. All we need to do is to give it some space in our routine and start doing it without questioning our feelings. Because once you suspect if you should do it or not, your mind comes up with creative reasons to rescue you from the hard work. Giving it space and not questioning it when the time comes is the trick here. Learn to trick your mind before it tricks you!

However, if the mind has already begun tricking you with its reasons, the only way to stop it is by posing the right questions. Divert the self-talk filled with feelings of "I don't feel like doing it," "I will do it later," "It's not that urgent," "It's too boring," "I feel like sleeping" to questions addressing the real issues. Instead of asking yourself whether you shall do it now or not, ask yourself, "Why should you be doing it?" "What will you get?" "What are the benefits of doing it instantly?" "Why did you add it to your routine in the first place?". These questions address the purpose, and when your purpose is strong enough to overpower the feelings, there is no question of procrastination.

To fight procrastination immediately, here's a workable idea. Divide the work you have been postponing into two different categories: Those which you have to do in any case and those for which you have a choice. Generally, we are not genuinely looking forward to doing all the work we have. We want to get rid of at least some of them. That's the trigger point. If you don't want to do the work and have a choice, better eliminate it. We usually have too much on our list either because we cannot say no or because we are bad at delegation. If you are doing something because of your inability to say no or inability to delegate properly, cut it off. Take the required action, and do not think of it again. That way, you can eliminate more than one-third of your work. From the rest of it, find the ones that need immediate attention and add it to your schedule. Don't think you will do it when you feel like it. Instead, assign a specific time and finish it by staying true to your words.

Action Challenge: *Allocate a specific time to one major work you have been procrastinating. Start doing it without questioning the feeling when the time arrives.*

CHOICES

CHAPTER NINE

USE YOUR MORNING ENERGY

We are in our best form in the mornings. A good night's sleep revitalizes our body and braces us for the hustle and bustle of life. Our body recovers when we sleep. The brain consolidates memories and deletes unwanted information. It restarts our system, making us ready to churn out. But sadly, the energy spike in the morning lasts only for a few hours. As the day passes, our energy level decreases and thereby our concentration and focus.

Lee Iacocca, the Chairman of Chrysler, shared how he learned early in life to use his concentration on essential activities for a brief specified period. During his college days, he used to tell himself, "I'm going to give this my best shot for the next three hours. And when those three hours are up, I'll set this work aside and go to the movies".[9.1] Through this simple but effective way, Lee focused all his will on the task at hand for the time he set for it and disburdened his mind off the job the moment he finished with it.

It does not matter what you do with the rest of your time if you can completely concentrate on your priorities when it's time. Ideally, mornings are the best time to allocate your energy to these priorities. Considering the fact that our energy is a limited resource, it's indispensable to make the most of it. It does not make sense to waste it on mundane tasks. We should use this energy spike for things of grave importance and tasks of great difficulty. It is wiser to direct it to things that require an intelligent and creative state of mind. Jeff Bezos, the founder of Amazon, solemnly schedules all his brainstorming meetings before noon. He says, "By 5 p.m., I'm like, I can't think about that today. Let's try this again tomorrow at 10 a.m.". Now, that's a man who knows the gravity of morning energy.

Most people wake up to the buzz of an alarm only to snooze it and doze off again. It's a war with lethargy every morning. Sound sleep is required to keep your body and mind rested. It's not the sleep timings that matter the most. It's the quality of sleep that makes all the difference. You may wake up at 9 a.m. or 9 p.m., and your body will still get rejuvenated to the same extent provided you had a pleasant sleep. So, it's okay if you can't wake up at 6 a.m. or earlier. But what's essential is that every morning, as soon as you wake up, you use this spark for your most valuable task, and you treat it with utmost care. Wondering, then why do most people, like Benjamin Franklin, preach "Early to bed, early to rise, makes a man healthy, wealthy and wise"? Keeping aside the morning cosmic energy, the most obvious reason is that the early hours are generally free from distractions. Waking up early gives you enough quiet time to think, strategize, understand, and bring clarity into life. Nevertheless, nothing could go wrong if you can wake up late and stay free from distractions. If you could use your energy spike for the right thing, then the time of the hour carries no weight.

Some of you might already have morning rituals like meditation, reading, affirmations, exercises, prayer, etc. That's terrific. You must be having a great start. Nonetheless, it would be exceptional if you could follow up your morning routine with the most challenging/creative/demanding part of your work. Treat the initial two to three hours after you wake up as the most sacred hours of your day. But are you left with time for anything else after your morning rituals? If you had to choose between your morning rituals and work, which one would you choose? Most people would prefer the morning rituals. At least, that is what they believe is expected of them for a lustrous life. I would be outright cast away if I tell you to choose your work over your morning rituals. Without any offense to this custom, I want to remind you that life is an assortment of trade-offs. You cannot always do the ideal thing. You would have to do the right thing at times. It's not easy for everyone to follow their morning ritual, have a healthy diet, look fit, spend time with family, and at the same time thrive at work. Trying to accomplish everything that comes your way is excruciating. Ascertain and accept your limitations. Skip the rituals if required to direct your morning energy into your dreams or needs. Though it would be good to add a few minutes of exercise/meditation/yoga in your morning routine, don't beat yourself up for it if you can add it in the later hours. After all, rituals are there to aid our life, not to inhibit it.

Automatizing your mornings can give you leverage in optimizing your time and energy. It can spare you the wastage of time caused due to avoidable deliberations. Once you have a fixed routine, you would be at it without much thought. Make it a point not to exhaust your limited time and energy on WhatsApp/Email/SMS until you conclude the work that needs this energy the most. Jim Kwik, one of the well-known brain trainers, says, "touching your phone in the first hour of your morning rewires your brain for distraction. It trains you to be reactive".[9.2] Morning is the time when you can naturally be very productive without extra effort. That's because when you wake up, your mind is devoid of the thoughts that get accumulated as the day passes. It is free of numerous information coming your way through WhatsApp, news, or conversations. When it's free from this data, its ability to focus naturally increases. The only effort you need to put is in starting what you have decided.

Before you sleep, decide on what task you will do the moment you wake up. Have things prepared the night before. Say you want to work on a project, set your laptop, and the documents on your work table the night before. Say you want to practice guitar, leave it at the designated place beforehand. In the morning, brush your teeth, and go straight for the task without accessing your phone. Spend at least an hour or two on the most challenging job and then do the chores. Practically, it's not always possible to leave off your morning responsibilities. Some of you might be required to prepare breakfast or get the kids ready for school, and you can't compromise on that front, but one thing you can surely do is get into the work as soon as possible. You may wake up early to set aside some time for yourself, or you may finish off your responsibilities in the least possible time and get to work.

Also do not make the mistake of starting your day with an easy task. I agree it seems comforting, but getting down to a difficult task after you have exhausted your energy would retard your efficiency, which is much needed for tasks requiring cognitive abilities. Research published by Harvard Business School says, "As individuals experience higher levels of load, they select easier tasks. Although it continues to have a positive impact on short-term performance, there are limits as there are diminishing returns to the gain".[9.3] The selection of a more manageable task, of course, aids short-term performance, but it indeed harms the total work you want to get done. Time could be unlimited, but energy is a finite resource. Depleting it on simple engagements could cost you your success. Channeling it to difficult tasks is the best way forward. Physically easier tasks like cleaning your house, packing your bag, and mentally easier tasks like replying to your mails, planning for a trip, could be done at a later hour without much effect on your efficiency.

Ideally, it's better to start your day with challenging tasks. However, it's okay to start with the easy ones once in a while. That way, you would see some progress even on an arid day. Nevertheless, it's always advisable to put your morning energy to the best use. Some of you might be thinking, "but I don't feel like working any time." The best way to handle this feeling is by following The Five Second Rule by Mel Robbins. She asserts that the trick to get to work is to move your body within five seconds of getting an instinct. When you don't physically move your body within five seconds, your brain kills your instincts with its reasons. Five seconds is the key here. Just get into action within five seconds before your thought train starts, and you would be able to finish any work you take on. Count 5-4-3-2-1 and boom! You would be into it before you could even notice.

Action Challenge: Decide the amount of time you will dedicate every day to the most challenging task just after you wake up. Save yourself from distraction by postponing the usage of your phone and chores until done. You may decide upon a time as short as thirty minutes to as long as five hours a day.

CHAPTER TEN

WHAT'S MORE PRODUCTIVE? BREAKS OR NO BREAKS?

Researchers and experts disagree on the exact duration of our attention span. Each one has a different theory, not in consensus with others from their domain. But underneath all such findings, there is one thing common: Human brains cannot function optimally by working continuously for a prolonged period. Once the attention is exhausted, we end up feeling bored and weary.

Breaks are scientifically proven to optimize cognitive performance. They provide a necessary pause in our activity, give a whole new dimension, a fresh burst of energy, and help us overcome mental exhaustion. When we resume the task after a break, we restore vigor, enhance concentration, add enthusiasm, and attain a more coherent mind than when we took off. It gives us a different perspective and an improved finesse to start again with a new drive. Our body needs to get moving every few minutes to work in its best form. To be productive, we should never forgo our breaks. Instead, we should master the ability to work a little longer before we take breaks.

Most of you might have heard that our body sleeps in cycles. One cycle typically lasting for ninety minutes. But do you know the same scientist who discovered sleep cycles also found that our body works in a rhythm of ninety minutes, even during wakefulness? Our body reaches its peak performance zone once every ninety minutes and experiences fatigue at the end of each cycle. The author of "The Way We're Working Isn't Working," Tony Schwartz shares he deliberately works in intervals of ninety minutes. He starts to work early in the morning, eats his breakfast in the first break, goes for a run in the second, and has his lunch in the third. These three cycles of ninety minutes each day were enough for him to write a book in less than six months. Before he knew this science, his previous books took more than a year, despite working for ten to twelve hours a day. [10.1]

Our body can perform in its best form if we mold our working style as per these cycles. Instead of working for longer hours, work for ninety minutes uninterrupted and take a short break for twenty minutes between each cycle. However, if you have a shorter attention span, you may start with twenty minutes of the productive session followed by a break of five minutes. As you get a hold of this routine, gradually increase your productive session's duration to ninety minutes but never more than that.

Barry Schwartz, an American psychologist, says, "during the day, we move from a state of alertness progressively into physiological fatigue approximately every ninety minutes. Our bodies regularly tell us to take a break, but we often override these signals and instead stoke ourselves up with caffeine, sugar, and our emergency energy reserves — the stress hormones adrenaline, noradrenaline, and cortisol".[10.2]

A short break of ten to twenty minutes in length is usually enough to refuel our brain with the performance vigor provided we spend it the right way! What we do in a break matters more than how long a break lasts. To rejuvenate yourself in the least amount of time, move out from your workspace, and detach yourself from the work you were doing. Physical activities like stretching, mild exercise, and taking a brief walk can tremendously enhance the quality of your breaks.

Getting our body moving has diverse effects on elevating our mood. It improves our blood circulation, breaks the monotony, and gets us ready for what's to come. A group of researchers recently conducted a study on the effects of interruptions on prolonged sitting. They divided the participants into three parts. Group one worked uninterrupted for six hours except for toilet breaks. Group two took a walk for thirty minutes before the start of six hours, and worked uninterrupted until the end. Group three took a treadmill walk for five minutes after every passing hour. It was found that Group three, office workers who were interrupted by five minutes of moderate-intensity treadmill walk, performed significantly better than the other two groups. The participants in the group felt more energy and vigor. The inclusion of walking improved their mood, decreased feelings of fatigue, and made them feel less hungry without impacting their cognitive performance.[10.3]

Our brain functions more efficiently after a brief physical session, especially when it is followed by a long session of physical inactivity. But to our dismay, activities like watching videos, playing games on the cellphone, checking social media feeds, and clearing mailboxes seem interesting. However, they happen to add to the weariness from work. Numerous scientists agree with each other that breaks require a sense of disconnectivity. Obviously, nobody designed our smart-phones with that in mind. If the disconnection is not our option, the least that we could do is to move around while glaring at digital screens. Walk while we talk/play/chat/watch. Considering the sedentary lifestyle that most of us follow, a brief walk during our break-time could do a little but much-needed help to our productivity.

Even on a long break, completely disentangle yourself from the task. Create a mental as well as a physical barrier between you and your job. Make sure to enjoy the holiday. Make it worth spending the time. Don't just buzz around, instead enjoy every moment of it. You could do something that energizes your body. Try activities that refuel your body or spend your time relaxing. Sleeping, napping, walking, healthy snacking, swimming, outdoor sports are some of the right options to go for in your breather time. These activities increase your willpower and leave you with a fresh burst of energy.

Don't take breaks just for the sake of taking a break, which means don't hang out with people you don't like, don't go to places you don't cherish, don't just lie around and think that tomorrow you will get back to normal. Primarily, detach yourself from your worrisome life. Disconnect yourself from the digital world. Choose to do something that rekindles your spirit. While on a break, only go for parties you enjoy, only meet people you think you will have a good time with, only go for trips you will love to be a part of, and only play sports that will give you a real thrill. Never compromise on your choices. Because when you do, you might end up being unsatisfied even after a long time out.

Small and extended breaks are both as important as action. The society we live in has made us accustomed to thinking that a seventy hour work week is the commandment. Though it works for Elon Musk, it may not work for us. We all need frequent breaks in between our work schedules. If we don't rest well, we can't produce more. You could beat the life out of yourself by working for ten hours a day. Still, the marginal value addition would be relatively minimal. I would also like to point out that if you are taking breaks seriously, it's also essential to follow your work sessions sincerely. Take breaks to enhance your productivity and not to escape work. In the end, it's all about how efficiently you work and how well you energize your body in your break time. The better you manage your energy by taking good breaks, the more productive you will be.

Action Challenge: *Pledge: I will do breathwork/take a walk/take a break for _______ minutes after every _______ minutes of work.*

YOU ARE WHAT YOU EAT

Would you believe if I say your chances of accepting an unfair but profitable monetary deal increases after having a low carb, high protein breakfast? Sounds insane, right? However, research backs it. To conduct the experiment, researchers made their participants play a one-shot UG game through which they were offered monetary deals. The catch was, if they felt the deal was unfair, they could punish the offeror by rejecting their offer, which also meant they (the player) receive nothing. The participants had to choose between punishing the offerer or accepting a one-sided deal, defeating their ego.

The results showed twenty-four percent of the participants who ate low carb, high protein breakfast rejected the offer. In contrast, fifty-three percent of the high carb, low protein group rejected the offer, showing increased social punishment behavior.[11.1] The log\ic behind the choice is simple. Carbohydrates increase blood sugar level which heightens emotions. Does this mean we should eat more protein to be productive? No. That's not my point.

I want you to focus on the fact that food can alter our behavior. But, for so long we had been eating just to kill our hunger. How many of us had thought that food on our plate can impact our minds? I say, when drugs and alcohol can change our behavior, why would a glass of juice or a hamburger not? There is enough evidence to show that our thoughts and emotions are affected by the food we eat. Some foods boost our negative emotions, while some boosts our cognitive abilities.

Our gut is known as "the second brain." The enteric nervous system present in our gut continually sends data to our brain through sensory receptors. Trillions of bacteria present in our stomach responsible for our mood, feelings, and emotions, generate these data. Our diet determines the bacteria that goes and gets processed in our gut. The food we eat contains both good and bad bacteria. Good bacteria are responsible for positive feelings and good cognitive performance. Bad bacteria are responsible for our mood swings, nausea, faulty decision making, and addictions.

Our energy level is highly dependent on the food we eat. A half-full stomach contains the perfect amount of food not to make us feel tired or lethargic. The Indian Mystic Sadhguru says most of our diseases would go away if we reduce our food intake by fifty percent. Indeed, research has found our brain performs better on an empty stomach. When we feel hungry, our body produces hunger hormones known as ghrelin. The little known fact is, this hormone also increases the hippocampus's neurogenesis, apart from making us feel hungry. Hippocampus is a part of the brain responsible for learning and memory. An empty stomach increases ghrelin production, which decreases cognitive aging by building new neural pathways. For a long time researchers thought new neurons cannot be formed in adulthood. However, with new research it's clearly evident that it's possible and an aging brain can recover its lost neurons.[11.2]

With these facts, it does not mean you should start fasting, but it certainly means you should choose your meal size and frequency consciously. Another way to improve your brain's capacity through food is by eating more servings of fresh fruits and vegetables. It increases eudaemonic well-being, curiosity, and creativity.[11.3] Snacking on a salad or a fruit during a short break also makes you more willing to return to the current work than junk food. The right combination of carbohydrates, proteins, and fats, along with a good portion of raw fibrous food divided into two to three meals a day, can work wonders. Various studies show that simple carbohydrates like processed sugar and refined starches elevate the blood sugar almost instantly, making our blood sugar level spike. Nonetheless, the blood sugar drops down almost as dramatically too. This rapid rise and fall of blood sugar levels leave us irritable, lethargic, and cranky. That's the prime reason why many people have cut down on processed sugar despite not having any health issues. If you ask a doctor, they will tell you that the sugar you eat starts getting digested in your mouth. If you chew your food properly, you are reducing the effort done by enzymes to break down the food in your intestine, as, besides feeding the brain, most of our energy is used in trying to digest the food. Ironically, digestion is the only process that releases energy in our body. The breakdown of food in our stomach releases energy, which gets absorbed through the intestines. Even though all energy discharged by various compounds is the same, how our body processes this energy, and nutrients may differ. Hence, it becomes crucial for us to pay attention to the source of these nutrients.

Athletes like Venus Williams, Jackie Chan, Arnold Schwarzenegger, Lewis Hamilton, and many others have shifted to plant-based diets to increase their energy levels. Olympic Cyclist Dotsie Bausch attributes her success in the 2012 Olympics to her shift towards a vegan diet. She won the Silver medal despite being ten to twenty years older than her competitors. She took up veganism due to ethical reasons fearing that it might reduce her energy level, but it did the opposite. Within a short span, she noticed that because of her new diet her energy levels and muscle recovery process has dramatically improved.

Start to observe your body's reaction to the food you intake. Give reasonable attempts to understand your irritation levels, anger, and mood swings due to your lifestyle choices. It would be hard at first, as small changes don't seem to reflect instantaneously. But stick with the plan and soon you will be able to distinguish between what is good and bad for your performance. One sorted way you can improve your productivity is by eliminating processed sugar from your diet. Yes, you read it right. Think of one reason why every packed item you eat contains sugar? It makes sense for cold drinks, flavored yogurts, and cereals to have sugar. For the time being, let's assume that a salty snack might also need sugar to improve the taste. But why do items like vitamin water, soup, ketchup, and sausages contain sugar? Around seventy-four percent of packaged food we eat contains sugar.[11.4] If you are happy to see that an item in your hand doesn't have sugar as an ingredient, let me tell you there are sixty-one different names given for sugar on food labels.[11.5]

There can be only one reason food companies add sugar to every food item apart from its purpose to improve taste - sugar works as an appetizer. It makes you want more. It triggers your brain and makes you addicted. I hope you have heard of that famous rat experiment. Scientists fed a group of rats a similar amount of cocaine and sugar every day. Later, when the rats had to choose between both options, almost all rats chose sugar over cocaine.[11.6] That's how powerfully addictive sugar is.

It isn't just addictive. Processed sugar is one of the most consumed dangerous food substances available today. It does not only add extra pounds to your body. It increases the risk of heart attack, diabetes, obesity, cancer, aging, and Alzheimer's, to name a few. The human body doesn't need processed sugar. It gets enough of it from fresh fruits and vegetables. Every natural food we eat contains sugar in some form. There is no need for additional sugar to complete our dietary requirements. Moreover, beware of different names. If it isn't coming from fresh fruits and vegetables, consider it bad.

My friend, Arya, recently went to a psychiatrist. She was having a hard time overcoming her emotions from the last two years because of a toxic relationship with her boyfriend. To everyone else, it seemed very easy for her to move on. She had a well to do family, great friends, and sound financial condition. Still, her overthinking kept dragging her into the pitfall. During her counseling sessions, her psychiatrist heard her story and asked her to follow a specific routine strictly. To be precise, she was asked to include meditation, yoga, exercise, face-to-face conversation with a friend everyday, fifteen minutes of sun exposure, spending time on her hobby, consuming superfood, vitamin B, Omega-3, and to avoid high fat and sugary foods in her routine. This basic routine, along with vitamin supplements and one medicine for anxiety, was her treatment. Isn't her prescription normal, and what is generally expected of a person? This advice to eat well, move more, and build genuine relations is anyway what everybody should be doing. It is so apparent.

Negative emotions are nothing but some hormone getting released in your body as per the food you are eating, the lifestyle you are following, and conversations you are having. Moreover, the psychiatrist specifically told Arya to avoid sugary and fried foods due to their propensity to escalate negative feelings and emotions.

When I was a child and had no understanding of the marketing world, I used to think, "Why would companies sell us something that isn't good for our health? The product must be good. Maybe people unnecessarily doubt the intentions of big corporations". Being a kid, I saw everyone as kind-hearted. As I grew up, I realized the world isn't so idealistic as I wanted to believe. As I read more about marketing, I understood how easy it is to play with the psyche of people; how easy it is to build a positive or negative image of anything in people's minds.

Nutritionist Andy Bellati says, "It's important for Americans to know that many health organizations receive funding from companies and trade groups that are not in line with health and how that affects recommendations." To name a few, American Diabetes Association, American Cancer Society, American Heart Association, Susan G Komen

(Breast cancer Organisation), etc., are sponsored by companies that display a clear conflict of interest. If that's not enough, the USDA recommendation committee is also funded by companies like McDonald's, American Meat Institute, Dannon, CocaCola, Kelloggs, Chocolate Council, Kraft, Campbell, Hershey's, M&M, Snack Food Association, etc. Thinking that this funding won't impact the USDA recommendations is insane.

A wrong recommendation may not wholly alter our food choices, but it can definitely alter the amount and frequency of our consumption and thereby our mood, health, and performance. Let's take some responsibility on our side and break this pattern of getting caught up by bad recommendations and poor eating habits. Let's reset the perspective we have towards food.

Action Challenge: *For the next forty five days, do not eat more than seventy-five percent of your stomach's capacity. Our stomach has the ability to reduce or increase its size depending on the quantity of food it gets. Give it some time and it will shrink its size.*

CHAPTER TWELVE

ADDING TO THE HOURS

Can you think of something common between Leonardo da Vinci, Nikola Tesla, Buckminster Fuller, Winston Churchill, Thomas Jefferson, and Bruce Lee? No, I am not talking about their eminence. It's about a lifestyle choice most of us ignore to follow. These famous personalities are champion proponents of napping and polyphasic sleeping. They advocated napping multiple times a day for smaller intervals. Some of them were even famous for sleeping less than two hours a day, all in the form of naps. This sleeping style is called polyphasic sleeping, a sleep pattern followed by eighty-five percent of the mammals.

The principal idea of polyphasic sleeping is to sleep several times a day for short periods. A simple polyphasic sleep includes four to six hours of sleep at night and an afternoon nap of one to two hours. The most challenging sleep pattern consists of a twenty-minute nap after every four hours of staying awake. If you do the math, you get to stay awake for more than twenty hours every twenty-four hours. That's eleven more years of staying awake than usual in a seventy-year lifespan! In the pre-industrialization era, there were no hard and fast rules for sleep and work timings. People slept as per their convenience. But today, taking a nap multiple times a day is not a workable idea. However, napping once a day is certainly possible. Indeed, it's a boon. In some professions, where sleeping for a whole night is not viable and compromising cognitive abilities is not an option, napping comes to the rescue. To improve job performance and safety on a space shuttle, NASA conducted thorough research on napping. They divided the commercial airline pilots flying between Japan and the USA into two groups. One group took a nap during the flight, and the other stayed awake. Over six days of study, it was found that pilots napping twenty-six minutes in the cockpit improved alertness by fifty-four percent and performance by thirty-four percent. Napping improved their reaction time and working memory, a memory function responsible for the temporary storage of information.[12.1]

Many companies like Google, Uber, Cisco, P&G, and Samsung encourage employees to take naps during their break time. Japan, the poster child of productivity, encourages all of its citizens to take regular naps. Taking a nap in coffee shops, bookstores, and parks is a widespread phenomenon in Japan. Another study conducted by Dr. Sara Mednick found that napping could lead to improved performance equivalent to sleep. During her research, she made the participants learn a variety of texture patterns. Then, one group of participants took a nap while the other stayed awake. The group that took an hour of nap containing both slow-wave sleep (SWS) and rapid eye movement (REM) performed significantly better on recalling texture patterns. They tested the participants further after a good night's sleep to ensure both the groups are well-rested before the next test. Yet, they found no change in their performance. Both groups' performance did not improve much even after eight hours of sleep, proving that a nap is as good as a night of sleep for learning. [12.2]

The same research also showed that irrespective of the nap's duration, naps that include slow-wave sleep and REM sleep, improve performance significantly. The study also indicates that though napping with SWS without REM sleep can maintain performance level, it isn't enough to escalate performance remarkably. To improve your learning significantly, the inclusion of rem sleep in naps is vital.

Slow-wave sleep is nothing but deep sleep. And REM sleep occurs just before wakefulness. It's a part of sleep where we watch dreams. In REM sleep, the body is paralyzed while the brain is as active as it is during wakefulness. With that, all I mean to say is, you should take naps in the coziest place you can find to reach these sleep phases in the shortest amount of time.

Dr. Sara Mednick, in her book, 'Take a Nap! Change Your Life' cites an array of reasons for napping. She shares napping boosts our decision making, accuracy, creativity, mood, and perceptions; fights off diseases like migraine, heart attack, and diabetes; flattens our bottom line and helps us lose weight; improves our stamina and of course makes us feel good.[12.3] She also considers it better than drinking coffee as it keeps us alert without reducing your retention power.

Brian Halligan, CEO of HubSpot, never misses his afternoon nap. He says, "Some of my best ideas I've had are when I'm kind of falling in and falling out of sleep, and it's like that eureka moment."[12.4] Sleeping during work is a bit frowned upon and seen as a sign of laziness. But in real terms, napping actually helps you outperform. It instantly refreshes your mind and gives it a fresh start. So, whenever you feel particularly tired or mentally exhausted between an intense brainstorming session, taking a nap is a great idea.

There is nothing better than a nap to rejuvenate yourself in the least possible amount of time. Just a fifteen-minute nap can restore your energy. It can make your body feel like you have woken up from hours of sleep and fends off your fatigue. You will be surprised to find out that the extent to which you feel energized after a nap, is quite similar to what you feel in the morning after a goodnight's sleep. If you have not tried it, you would never believe it. When I first heard it from my professor, I did not take him seriously and tried it only after he suggested it for thirty times. These days I make sure I nap once a day to recharge myself.

Here's the golden tip to make the most use of napping. Divide your days into two parts and separate it with a thirty minutes nap. If you have two priorities, it's a good idea to tackle them in two different parts of the day, separated by a nap. A thirty-minute nap is sufficient to give you enough energy to make you feel like a new day has started. Use the division wisely and make the most of it by using the energy spike for essential activities.

"Nature has not intended mankind to work from eight in the morning until midnight without that refreshment of blessed oblivion which, even if it only lasts twenty minutes, is sufficient to renew all the vital forces... Don't think you will be doing less work because you sleep during the day. That's a foolish notion held by people who have no imaginations. You will be able to accomplish more. You get two days in one — well, at least one and a half,"

Winston Churchill

No matter what style of sleep you choose and how often you nap, keep in mind treating the energy after your nap is sacred. Spend it only on essential activities because these patterns work when you work. The energy spike and clarity of mind you get after a nap don't last forever, making it all the more important to spend only on prime activities. Develop the habit of napping for a short while before dipping your hands into challenging tasks. It will not only leave you calmer and relaxed but will give you a much-needed boost after the day's work. It would clear off the psychological clutter, the emotional dramas, the thoughts of the unnecessary, the pointless worries, and would let you direct your brainpower into the task at hand.

Action Challenge: *Take a twenty minute nap every afternoon/evening for the next one week preferably before an hour of intense work. Be observant of its benefits for a week. You may also take a longer nap, including slow-wave sleep and rapid eye movement, by sleeping in a cozy, dark, and peaceful environment.*

CHAPTER THIRTEEN

ACCOUNTABILITY ENHANCES PERFORMANCE

"Lack of direction, not lack of time, is the problem. We all have twenty four hour days."

-Zig Ziglar

People do not lack motivation. They lack direction. You would not have picked this book had you lacked motivation. Many of us have the motivation and dedication, but we rarely have the right guidance, and rarely someone helps us cross the bridge. If you leave the winning Olympic basketball team to practice without a coach for the next Olympics, there's a high probability the team would lose. The team would not lose because of the lack of capability. It would lose because of a lack of direction and oneness.

Harshit Pandey, one of my friends, was known for his callous attitude. But after he met his mentor, he turned into the most desirable man in society. The mere presence of an officer of the Indian Army willing to give him good suggestions just for two months turned him into a man from a spoiled brat.

Before he met his mentor, he had no direction and was casually passing through life. He was moving aimlessly, not acknowledging the potential he had. His mentor recognized his capability and started giving him daily guidance. He established a system for his physical training and spent time sharing his stories. He never told him what to do. But he gave him personal examples and explained what, why, and how of everything he did. Harshit soon started to capitalize on his ideas and brought the changes he couldn't have thought of himself. Had he not met his mentor, his life would have stayed the same. His mentor unleashed his dormant confidence and made him realize that he was capable.

If you have a good mentor, then you are blessed with a guardian angel. Life is a thorny path. But the presence of the right mentor can help one glide through those thorns. One right advice when you are ragging the puck in your life, one right direction when you are up in the air, and one right suggestion before you turn down something, can change your life radically. It's an old saying, "Two heads are better than one." If one gets stuck, the other pulls out with force. A mentor is that force that can get you out of your most challenging situations or can help you overcome your fears. A mentor epitomizes knowledge, experience, and understanding. The right mentor could help you transform your monkey talk to money-that-talks. Even the most successful turn to their mentors in times of need. Bill Gates considers his relationship with Warren Buffet more than just friendship. He has turned to him for advice on various occasions. Mark Zuckerberg had Steve Jobs, Steve Jobs and Steve Wozniak had Mark Markkula, Michael Bloomberg had Billy Salomon, and Oprah Winfrey had Maya Angelou. Some of these alliances lasted for years, while some were temporary. Still, no matter what, these people continued to find and hold onto mentors despite their tremendous success and knowledge on their subject. They knew that it's always good to have a guide. Though they made their own success, they acknowledge others' contributions that added to their pursuit.

While looking for a mentor, find someone who has walked the path, not just talked the path. Having someone who has already trudged the path makes the job much easier. It helps to gain insights into the nuances of future events and gives a chance to be fully prepared for what might come. Moreover, you get the much-needed network and skillset. Richard Branson, the founder of Virgin Group, sought mentorship from Freddie Laker, founder of Laker Airways, while starting his airline company Virgin Atlantic. He relied on Freddie's knowledge and experience of creating one of the earliest low-cost, no-frills airline companies. Laker not only shaped Branson's vision, but he also introduced him to the strengths of his competition.

Having a good mentor decreases the chances of committing honest mistakes and, at the same time, increases the speed of decision making. Generally, when we face a situation or find it challenging to make a decision, we talk to our friends and seniors, and most of the time, take their advice and stick with it. But do you think they are the best ones to guide you in the right direction? Are their lives really happening in the manner they desired? I have made numerous mistakes myself by listening to random advice. Be very decisive of the people you trust. Take advice only from people who are worthy.

Life unfolds itself with every decision we take and every outcome we stake. There are multiple paths in front of us. The one we happen to choose makes the difference. We can neither walk each path and choose the best one nor can we ever look back and judge where the other paths would have led, which makes choosing the right path quite unnerving. The right mentor can help us go past this uncertainty and make the best decision standing where we are. We are undoubtedly the makers of our lives, but even the makers need a great team to create a masterpiece. A mentor is a critical player in such a team who can complete the jigsaw puzzle with the required pieces.

We have always turned to someone in times of need. We seeked advice from different people in different situations, and all those people have acted as our mentors. Though we never tried to name these relations as mentorship, it existed. Since childhood, we have counted on our teachers for guidance, our seniors for suggestions, and our parents and relatives for important decisions. However, in the most important endeavors of our life, we are on our own. When we need suggestions the most, we don't know whom to ask. We know these endeavors require critical judgments and can unfold great things with our decisions. Yet, we ignore the significance of having a mentor.

When you know where you stand, you have a better chance of winning. A man who knows his shortcomings and strengths knows the area he needs to work on. It's important to distinguish between what you 'can' do and what you 'should' do. 'Can' and 'should' lead to two distinct streets. 'Can' is the right way to think when you seek your passion and purpose, while 'should' shall be given intense consideration in the process of execution. Humans are blessed with immense potential. All of us are born with similar characteristics that say we 'can' do anything and everything we come across. However, the larger question to ask is what one 'should' do? 'Can' is an array of opportunities, while 'should' is the one you are looking for. A good mentor can clarify these little dilemmas in a fraction of seconds.

Finding the right mentor might not be easy, as with every good comes bad, and it's your responsibility to be able to distinguish between those. Not every characteristic of a person should be modeled. Even the wisest and the brightest of all have a dark side. It may not be evident but is always part and parcel. Be cautious not to leave your life in anyone's hands. Even the ones that you consider your gods could mislead you when their dark side becomes your companion. This does not mean you should doubt your mentors. It only means that being cautious is always a safe bet.

Warren Buffet says, "You only have to do a very few things right in your life so long as you don't do too many things wrong." A mentor can help you do that. Choose someone experienced, well achieved, and more knowledgeable than you are. Make sure you have at least one mentoring session every month.

It is said that your mentor appears when you are ready for it. You need not find one. Indeed, when you are prepared to do what it takes and are open to learning, your mentor finds you. However, until that happens, it's a good idea to find an accountability partner. Joe Dumas says, "On good teams, coaches hold players accountable. On great teams, players hold players accountable".

According to Pearson's Law — when performance is measured, it improves; when performance is measured and reported back, the rate of improvement accelerates. Miracles happen when immediate feedback is given to people who have the desire to continually improve. Research done by The American Society of Training and Development (ASTD) shows that you have a sixty-five percent chance of completing a goal if you have an accountability partner. Also, you have a ninety-five percent increase in the chance of success if you interact with your accountability partner daily.

Often, I have felt, "I wish someone had told me this before." Whether it was when I was in school or college or was looking for a job, or was having fun in my life, there were countless occasions when I felt things could have been better. My actions and decisions could have been wiser if I had the right guidance, feedback, and someone to be accountable to.

Remember how you studied before a college test; how you worked hard when your boss's eyes were on you; and how beautifully you decorated your house when you invited someone for dinner. In all those events, you had someone to judge you and rate you, sometimes openly, sometimes silently. And you did all that for nothing but to leave a positive impression. Similarly, in life, we are more likely to stick to a commitment when we make ourselves accountable.

To find an accountability partner, look for someone who is trustworthy, honest, willing to act as your critique, and certainly not afraid to voice their opinion when need be. Use this peer pressure to your advantage as a tool to reach your goals. Both of you should be willing to coach each other and exchange positive and negative feedback. Someone bold enough, committed to getting better, cares for you, and is serious about personal development would be the best choice. Make sure to have someone you trust because if you won't trust your partner, why would you care to listen.

Agree to have a weekly feedback session where you can both discuss your achievements and shortfalls. Make each other accountable for those calls, and make sure you don't compromise on it even once. More importantly, be honest. It's essential to have a partner with whom you can discuss everything without the fear of being judged. It doesn't matter if your accountability partner is your spouse or a person you met yesterday as long as they match the requirements.

Action Challenge: Reach out to a friend right now who you think can turn out to be a good accountability partner. It's either now or never! Share the content written above and the workbook to acquaint him with the things you are looking for. Schedule a weekly call and get going. Utilize the workbook judiciously to follow an effective regime.

To access the workbook, refer to Part 5 - Accountability Report.

CHAPTER FOURTEEN

DEVELOPING THE RIGHT SKILLS

Who had thought Jack Ma's command over English would open his doors for becoming the richest man in China? At a very early age, he realized the importance of the English language. He worked as a tourist guide and learned most of his English from foreign visitors. As he had a good command over the language, the Chinese government asked him to assist as an interpreter and sent him to America to settle a pending government deal. That's when he got his chance to see the Internet. His friend showed him what the Internet was and said you could find anything over the web. Bewildered, he searched for a few words and got the results but found nothing when he looked for China. Disappointed to see his country not mentioned once, he asked his friend to build a web page about his small translation agency in China. Within a few hours, he received five emails from the US, Japan, and Germany. He was stunned by his discovery. This happened back then in 1994 when he did not even know what Email was. Realizing the impact the Internet can create in the world, he bought a computer, took it to China, left his job, and built China's first internet company 'China Pages.' It was an internet version of Yellow Pages in the English language. He later built what we know today as Alibaba. Had he not learned English or learned working over the Internet, he wouldn't have had today's success. You may never know what skills will prove to be the reason for your success, but one thing is sure that developing them will only turn out to be beneficial.

All skills can be developed, which is why they are called skills and not inherent talent. Oxford Dictionary defines skill as "the ability to do something well." You may not succeed in developing expertise into everything you come across but doing fine in most cases is always in your hand.

Let's be clear. You need a good skill set to do your job well. On one side of the number line, some masses earn a mere $100 a month, while on the other side, few make more than $1000000 a month. What would you choose if you need to give credit to one practical factor that decides where you stand on this number line? Would it be luck? Or would it be the parents you were born to or the university you studied in? Or the business idea you have? In his famous book "Think and Grow Rich," Napoleon Hill gives credit for everyone's success to their thinking. He says what you think materializes into reality. Even the book and the documentary "The Secret" explains how our thoughts alter our reality. Regardless of that, on a much practical side, you will find that these people have spent an enormous amount of time developing their skills. They attracted their skills by practicing hard on them. They are getting paid because of the skills they have. They have developed the talent that delivers higher output than those who stand at the front of the number line. They use the law of attraction, but along with it, they prepare themselves to be worthy enough to receive the energy.

Pratik Bathwal, a Chartered Accountant in my hometown, provides professional services and earns twice as much as his graduation class. When I asked him his mantra, he said he spends thrice the amount of time improving his caliber compared to the time he spends on executing his tasks. His daily routine inculcates more than five hours of work time for refining his skills and includes a minuscule amount of time on executing the tasks. He believes the ratio of time spent on learning to the time spent on execution shall never be less than two.

Being a practitioner, he has to look for new clients to sustain his earning, which is equally valid for his peers. But, unlike others, Pratik never compromises on sharpening his skills for money. He knows money will flow to him one day or the other if he sticks to his ratio of 2:1. Choosing to work with new clients is always a lucrative option for a beginner. Yet, Pratik did not trade off his choice of spending hours and hours on refining his competence. He always chose his long term goals over his short term goals. When his peers were busy executing the work, he was busy learning how to perform better.

I personally know many of his peers, and I can say they aren't less talented either. All of them started their practitioner's journey from scratch with almost similar skill sets. Yet, Pratik's choice of spending more than two third of his time working on his skills proved doubly fruitful to him. For all of us, the skill we need differs depending on the goals we have. It is essential to understand the right skills which will impact your work the most.

Donald Trump has many skills. From being an incredible deal maker to having great contacts to having a knack for hiring exceptional people to run a real estate business, he knows it all. But one thing that sets him aside from everyone else is his personal branding skill.

In the 1990s, Trump's business was having the worst time. He was forced to put his two excellent real estate properties, The Taj Mahal Hotel and his casino, into bankruptcy. He had to sell his other properties as well, yet he couldn't repay his debts. So in June 1995, he took his business public. The IPO got his company $1.2 billion. Donald personally got $82 million. Out of which, $52 million was used entirely to pay off his debt. Isn't it weird that people invested in an IPO to help him pay off his debt? Why would someone want to do that? Were they ignorant of the truth that his business was failing, or were they too mesmerized by Trump's image? Marketing is a game of perception, which Trump understands very well. People were aware that his accounts are weak, but the perception that Trump built on people's minds was hard to escape. The presidential election is another example of successful marketing. People did not vote for Trump's agenda. They voted for his brand. You need not have it all to be great at something. Some special skills are enough to get you going. Get them before it's late. Select the skills most relevant to you and focus on honing them to your best extent. Acknowledge the areas where your lack of a particular skill is bringing you down or hindering your progress.

Abraham Lincoln has said it well, "Give me six hours to chop down a tree, and I'll spend the first four sharpening the ax." Most of us do not like changes. We are so fearful of change that we fool ourselves into believing we are content with what we have. We do not try, not because we are happy, but because we have conceived in our mind that we have already lost the battle. We don't think beyond our current situation because we are sure we are only worthy of what we have achieved already. Being content is different while optimizing yourself is another side of the spectrum. Darren Hardy, in his book The Compound Effect, has explained how small, consistent daily habits over a long period compound and deliver massive results. He explains how a daily improvement of 0.1 percent compounds to a twenty-six percent annual personal growth rate. Doesn't that sound great? Are we so occupied with the circumstances that we can't even afford to improve ourselves by a mere 0.1% a day? Think well before you answer. This improvement takes bare minimum effort.

Self-optimization is one of the best daily goals to have. Take small specific areas as a challenge to work on. It can be your skill, knowledge, emotion, relationship, diet, or anything else. Take simple actions like speaking one extra line of appreciation to your team members, increasing exercise time by, say, three minutes, working on a project for a few additional minutes, or reading two more pages of a book. These activities don't take much effort if one is determined to play the game. One of the best batsmen in the world, Indian cricketer Virat Kolhi, says every time he goes into a practice session, he tries to improve himself, even if it's just by 0.1%.

The easiest way to analyze your growth is to check every day, whether you are better than yesterday. If the answer is yes, continue. If not satisfied, pace up. If the answer is no, admit the reality and take immediate, decisive steps. If it seems too hard to revive back, focus on reaching a neutral position. After all, non-negativity is also positivity. For a while, it's good to embrace that.

Steve Jobs fans must have heard- he had a reality distortion field, had good business acumen, believed in the integration of hardware and software, and had an edge on design. However, he had another mesmerizing skill that helped him make Apple successful. He had a charm which nobody could escape. He was so compelling that even his enemies believed he was his friend. He had the power to influence everyone he met within minutes. That's one of the crucial skills that has led him to crack amazing deals with various companies making him achieve what was seen as impossible by the world. To achieve more, we all need to realize that there isn't just one factor contributing to achievement. It's a combination of several skills. I doubt the magnitude of his success without the right combination of the skills mentioned above. Looking forward to the right combination of skills is impossible as dots can only be connected looking backward. However, it's still enough to start and acknowledge the current skills you need to improve to be better in your job right now.

Mark Cuban, a successful entrepreneur, and investor was learning Artificial Intelligence in 2020. He was taking python classes. He shared he had a book in his bathroom- Machine Learning for Idiots and has taken courses on Coursera. He wasn't aiming to be the best at it. He was learning to have the edge over the hottest technological advancement of the 21st century. He is betting highly on companies based on Artificial Intelligence. And he isn't alone. Most of the CEO's are today dipping their hands in AI. If these CEO's can take out time to learn new skills, why can't you?

Even if you think your skills are gifted, it remains your responsibility to build and rebuild them as time demands. Great leaders did not become great because they had everything. They became great because they diligently practiced leadership. They polished their skills with the changing scenarios. They were ready to adapt to the newest technologies, marketing models, designs, etc. They were prepared to learn, unlearn, and relearn.

Before recently, I never gave too much importance to unlearning and relearning. I couldn't realize how important it can turn out to be. I heard about it at various places but never considered it seriously. However, the recent market crash of 2020 explained to me an exceptional example of its relevance. During the turbulence in global financial markets by Covid-19, some of the investors went into panic selling while the smarter ones were accumulating stocks. There was another category of people who were making small profits by trading. These weren't technically traders, but speculators and were mostly trying their luck. They had been doing the same for forever. Though they knew that a long term investor wins the race, given a long time horizon and the bit-sized buying and selling in a volatile market wouldn't leave them with a 1000% return, which is possible when we invest with the guidelines of Warren Buffet and Benjamin Graham, they kept trading hoping for quick profits. Even after imparting the right knowledge, I had a hard time convincing people around me to do it the right way. I am not talking about full-time traders trading with specific skills of technical analysis and derivatives. I am talking about thousands of people who enter the stock market to speculate and try their luck. These categories of people include my friends, clients, and family members. They weren't entirely wrong in doing what they were doing, provided their experience and knowledge. However, despite being exposed to the right information, they weren't receptive. After all, how can they be when there is so much wrong information floating out there? That's when I realized the importance of unlearning and relearning. To leave everything you know already and start all over again. To be open to understanding that you can be wrong and you have been doing it all wrong. To learn to question the known and tapping into the unknown. To be willing to learn some of the skills from scratch so that in the end, you not just survive but also thrive.

Sometimes with the change of circumstance, our philosophies must also be changed. When we had first learned to do things a certain way, we did okay. But with the change of time and especially after you have realized that the olden methods wouldn't work, it's time to consider unlearning and relearning. The futurist, writer, and businessman Alvin Toffler says, "The illiterate of the 21st century will not be those who cannot read and write, but those who cannot learn, unlearn and relearn." As per the World Economic Forum, more than half of the workforce needs significant reskilling and up-skilling by 2022.[14.1] Given the pace of development and high expectations from employers, added with the contractionary business cycle, those who aren't proactive will find it very difficult to achieve their dreams in the coming years. With the growing population, high standard of living, and excessive competition, those who aren't ready to adapt will have a hard time fulfilling their expectations. With many jobs getting overtaken by machines, it has become more critical to embrace the skills that machines can't learn.

To lead a productive life, here are the four skills everyone shall acquire:

1. Leadership skills - to induce your people to make the best use of themselves.

2. Interpersonal skills - to bring harmony to your relations.

3. Hardcore work-related skill- to complete your tasks with ease and be recognized without deliberate effort.

4. Focus - to concentrate your mind on what's relevant and toss out the irrelevant.

To acquire new skills, the three most important things you need are- a good source of learning, consistency, and efficacious practice. If your learning source is terrible, you would probably lose interest even in an exciting subject. If you won't be consistent for enough time, an easy to acquire skill would also go out of your way. And if you do not expand your boundaries while practicing, your growth would be limited. These three factors are much more influential than your interest, method, companion, etc.

Richard Branson says, "If somebody offers you an amazing opportunity, but you are not sure you can do it, say yes – then learn how to do it later!". While joining their first company, a lot of people aren't rehearsed with the job at hand. The employer as well knows their employees would need training. These days, it's very common to major in a different subject and work in an entirely different industry. A fresher who joins at the lowest level in the company also climbs up the ladder and becomes the CEO. How do these people manage to do it? They learn it.

All skills can be developed, but not all of them will suit you. Everyone has their unique sweet spots. Find your sweet spot and develop different skills keeping in mind its suitability. If you hate persuasion, do not waste your energy on developing marketing skills. If you hate to sit for long hours, don't waste your time trying to learn to code. Finding the skills that may prove to be most beneficial can be formidable. However, accumulating good skills can always turn tables on your side somewhere sometime. You can't be sure what skills can prove valuable in the future, nor can you clearly foresee its vitality in a day to day life, but one thing you can surely do is keep adding them up in your mind.

Action Challenge: *Write down one skill you aim to learn in the next six months. Layout a plan and get the resources immediately.*

CHAPTER FIFTEEN

NO CRAP

Reuters' survey says, eighty-five percent of people in Brazil are concerned over what is real and fake when it comes to news on the Internet, followed by seventy percent in the UK and sixty-seven percent in the US and France. You will be aghast to know that some companies are incorporated explicitly with the agenda to spread fake news. In the past few decades, the objective of news has shifted from spreading awareness to catching attention for making higher profits. We all are well aware of how easy it has become these days to spread a rumor. The negative news is far more fascinating to most of us than positive news. Be it criticism, discouragement, or a nasty rumor. Our brains love to delve deeper and fantasize about the situation. It is called the "negativity bias." Money-minded news organizations are well aware of it. They dole out more negativity, and our brains start feeding on it. This can have a drastic impact on our behavior, decisions, and relationships. Very few of us can fully control our thoughts and emotions. I am sure you must have noticed your muscles getting strained while watching an action scene. We tend to feel as if we are the ones fighting when, in reality, we are sitting and eating popcorn. If you haven't noticed it, next time, pay attention to your friend while he is watching an action scene. Most of us go to a movie to escape from our monotonous routine. But did you notice that sometimes after a movie, you feel worked up rather than re-energized? Not every movie does that, but the plot of the movie has a fair amount of contribution towards how you feel at the end. Probably that's the reason why some people prefer light comedy movies instead of serious drama. Well, the point isn't who likes what. It's about how immensely immersed we are with seeing and hearing despite being physically disentangled. And it would be half-baked of you to think that needless disheartening stories and issues of your friends and your friend's friends wouldn't affect you.

In this technological world, any information, irrespective of whether you are interested, gets disseminated to you in a jiffy. However, an eagle's eye can bring to light that most of the information we encounter is impertinent to us. Though certain information relating to the current scenarios like climate change, terrorism, diseases, animal extinction, nutrition, etc., can be of concern to us, it's just another futile entanglement if we have no intention to act. Then why should we unnecessarily bombard our brains with this irrelevant data? It's fundamental to be aware. It's not essential to delve.

Once when I was at a relative's place, while we were getting ready for a party, my uncle watched cricket being dressed already. Looking at the interest with which he was watching, I said to my cousin, "It looks like he is a fan of cricket." To my revelation, my cousin said, "It's not like that. He watches cricket so that he can discuss it with his friends". I cannot call it a bad practice, but I wasn't expecting such a reply. If you notice, you will realize that most of us keep ourselves updated with political and economic news to not get side-lined in group talks. I have personally felt pressure on numerous occasions.

When the human species transpired, there was a lot less to know. However, in the past two decades, the dispersion of information has taken a new shape. Our brain is not conditioned to process this vast amount of data. It goes into denial. It starts to ignore information it can't handle, like solving the issue of ozone layer depletion, income inequality throughout the world, the spread of diseases, etc. It denies everything that produces too much stress knowing well enough that it's for real. Glad our brain functions this way. If it were not, we would have died thinking of all the issues humankind is facing. Fortunately, our brain only burdens itself with information that we can handle, like losing weight, waking up early, planning for retirement corpus, etc.

However, every piece of information has some or the other effect on us, at least more than we think. Those of us who dream frequently must be aware, how our dreams shape as per the recent data we received. Those who don't dream are equally swayed. Steve Jobs is well known for his reality distortion field. He was known to ignore the information, even facts, and focus his attention on his ongoing projects. On numerous occasions, he ignored personal issues to focus better on his professional life. It was to such an extent that when his girlfriend revealed the news she is pregnant, he ignored it completely, declaring it's not his child. Years later, he accepted his child. She's none other than Lisa Brennan Jobs. This is just one of the situations where Steve ignored reality not to let down his focus. Most of us do not dare to do this, nor is it morally right, yet focus is the key to massive success. But how do we achieve it? It's simple. Save your brain from getting exposed to unnecessary information. Be it gossip, news, unnecessary criticism, personal judgments, celebrity lifestyles, advertisement, etc. It's mostly of no use to us until and unless we have a vested interest.

Stop punishing your brain mindlessly by giving it unproductive data. Instead, nurture it with good books. Sharpen it with witty puzzles. Relax it with soothing music. If you like to keep yourself updated with the latest information, be judicious in choosing its source. Replace your radio/ television time with self-help podcasts and audiobooks. Stop hanging out with people bringing negative energy into your life. Cut off or limit your interactions with such people. Stop entertaining gossip. It's not taking you anywhere. Instead, it is making you fall into the pitfall of mediocrity. When mediocrity is your lifestyle, then success can never be your destiny!

Negativity is like your body fat. Easy to gain but tough to shed. Given the capacious spread of negativity, it's easier for our brains to relapse into it. The only way out is to stop your brain the second it starts fantasizing about it. Before your negative thought starts to take over your mind, replace it with a positive thought. Initially, you will find it difficult, but with practice, there will come a day when you would effortlessly handle such matters. If you find it too hard to replace your negative thoughts with positive ones, then the best way is to start moving. Fool your brain as it fools you. Start working, cooking, talking, watching, etc. Do whatever it takes to distract your mind from that thought. If you are a computer, your brain is the processor. Either you increase the RAM by doing meditation, yoga, and exercises, or you give the processor less information to process and let it assign its full energy to the significant areas.

Action Challenge: Write down one thing that is sucking your mental or physical energy. Replace it/ Reduce it/ Eliminate it. (Example: It can be your desk setup, social circle, poor delegation, news, etc.)

CHAPTER SIXTEEN

WHY DO YOU NEED TO MEDITATE?

How many seconds in a day are you operating with 100% awareness? How many seconds are you completely present in the moment? You are doing great if the number is in double digits! We are present minuscule of each second, very few moments, say while experiencing pain or enjoying the beauty of nature. The rest of the time, we are living in our head, in our self-created version of the world, entertaining the same thoughts hundreds of times like a broken tape record.

This brings me to the question: why does our brain even generate so many unnecessary thoughts, to be precise, more than 50000 thoughts a day? And why is it so tough to get rid of them?

Our thoughts are a result of our memories and sensory perceptions. We perceive thoughts when our brain generates the movement of chemicals or electrical signals between our neurons. However, apart from electrochemical reactions, we have one more thing that determines the number and frequency of thoughts we perceive. It's the chemical known as gamma-aminobutyric acid (GABA). It's an amino acid responsible for inhibiting unwanted thoughts. When it's present more in our body, it reduces the neuronal excitability and makes us calmer. It reduces the number of superfluous thoughts generated in our minds and keeps us at peace. That says why individuals suffering from stress and anxiety have lower GABA levels.

Today, stress-related problems are responsible for 60% to 90% of visits to the doctor accounting for the third highest health care expenditure after cancer and heart diseases. With the change of times, staying calmer is becoming tougher day by day. The problems creating these stresses aren't that big. It's our inability to handle them, which is causing these visits.

The good news is, we have a way out. A study at the Boston University School of Medicine found that participants who practiced yoga for twelve months increased their GABA levels by twenty-seven percent. [16.1] Other researchers have found a positive correlation between meditation and GABA levels. That says why meditation, yoga, and mindfulness are so much talked about these days. Almost every research justifies their positive effects on our health and stress levels.

When we were born, the first thing we did was to breathe. That is what has kept us alive. If you are a beginner and have never practiced meditation, start by focusing on every breath you take in and give out. Start with ten minutes of guided meditation. Although the perfect time to practice meditation as per Sadhguru, an Indian yogi are 3:40 a.m., 5:40-6:20 a.m./p.m. and 11:40-12:20 a.m./p.m., you may practice it anytime if the timings aren't suitable.

One misconception about meditation is, people think they should not think anything. That's not possible for beginners. Meditation doesn't require you to stop your thoughts. Instead, it requires you to be present to your thoughts. It needs you to acknowledge the ongoing thoughts and slightly shift your attention back towards noticing your breath. It's a practice to concentrate your attention on one thing for a specific amount of time.

Another easy way you can get yourself calmer is by practicing mindfulness. Mindfulness and meditation are slightly different. Meditation is practiced for a few minutes, while mindfulness is a continuous process of carefully observing your thoughts throughout the day. It demands you to pay absolute attention to the thoughts, emotions, sensations, and experiences occurring in the present moment without being judgemental.

Practicing mindfulness doesn't require you to sit and meditate. You can do anything and everything and yet be present to your current experiences. Start with observing your thoughts. Every moment, be aware of the dialogues going on in your mind. Do not judge them. But slowly bring them back to the present moment. To dwell deeper, experience the flow of energy in your body. We all are a collection of protons, neutrons, and electrons. This may be hard to understand, but with a conscious attempt, you will surely be able to feel your energy. Keep practicing it throughout the day and make it a habit.

When you are consciously aware of your thoughts, you can be more productive. Your awareness will keep bringing you back to the present moments and will help you focus more on your work. It will clear the clutter and will give you much-needed space for the work at hand. Research conducted by the University of California found that the students who took mindfulness training for two weeks improved their GRE score from 460 to 520. Thirty minutes of mindfulness meditation improved their working memory and reduced mind wandering.

Another research conducted by scientists of Columbia University on patients of medical centers in New York found that mantra meditation improved cardiac blood flow by twenty percent.[16.2] Mantra meditation, also known as transcendental meditation, is easier than other forms of meditation for beginners, as it only requires you to utter some words. If you find it too hard to convince yourself to utter words that have no meaning for you, let me tell you, mantra meditation doesn't work because of the meaning those mantras carry. They work because of the vibration it creates in our bodies. These vibrations can be easily felt by uttering the words suggested as mantras in a specific tone. Don't believe me? Try this out: Sit straight and speak "Aaaa" (as pronounced in Father) and stretch it for fifteen seconds. Put your palm on your chest, and feel the vibration.

Getting our blood flowing is extremely significant for our wellbeing. Whether you choose to meditate or you choose to exercise, if you can successfully limit your thoughts and get your body energized with good blood circulation, the choice won't matter.

When I was a child, I belonged to the lazy category. Almost everyone suggested that I exercise and eat vegetables. But who listens to others? I was my own boss. I liked to be lazy and loved myself that way. But my laziness had its costs. I looked dull, my skin was terrible, my hair was frizzy, I lacked energy, I had to study for longer hours compared to my friends, and lacked vigor. This story continued until I started eating fruits to look good and started walking to lose fat. My intention was never to boost my brain performance. I did it to look better. But when you do something good, you get more than one reward. Within a few months, I could feel the difference in my energy levels. My concentration improved, which was a significant problem during my childhood. I found myself accomplishing more things in the same amount of time. This became better and better as I started exercising. Today, even after a party, I am filled with energy when everyone else wants to sleep. My memory and attention span have got better. Most importantly, now I don't get tired quickly and can work effectively for longer hours.

All of this happened with tiny changes in my lifestyle. I decided to walk more and deliberately moved my body whenever possible. I did not do something out of the box, joined a gym, or went on a diet, but I took simple steps to change my habits. I started wearing sports shoes and took short walks with friends during lunch or snack breaks. I later started exercising just for ten minutes to get the blood flowing in my body. I started skipping randomly, mostly on my five minutes break between work.

Your brain needs continuous circulation of blood for optimal functionality. When the brain cells experience good blood flow, it becomes easier for it to make newer connections. Its functionality improves within seconds. Exercise helps in the production of a protein called GPLD1. Though this protein gets produced in the liver, it has positive effects in reducing the brain's aging effect and thus improves our learning and memory. A study at the University of British Columbia found that the size of the hippocampus, the brain part responsible for learning and memory, increased in women who did regular aerobic exercise for one year.[16.3] Researchers also claim that the risk of dementia can be reduced by thirty percent by regular exercise.

Exercise has always been suggested to be done in the morning hours. It's said it should be one of the first things in our daily routine. One of the primary reasons behind it is- it increases blood circulation, which increases our freshness and thereby our focus. It helps us make more informed and unemotional decisions by reducing our adrenaline and cortisol levels.

You need not do something severe to get the blood flowing. Do the easy ones. Find out what you are most comfortable with and jump on it whenever possible. Moving your body is essential. How and where you move do not matter much. Don't run behind what others are doing. Stick with what suits you better. Remember your motive and dive into your favorites. Running, skipping, dancing, walking, swimming, yoga, meditation, anything is acceptable, provided the goal is achieved.

The benefits of exercise, meditation, and mindfulness are numerous. Various research has proved that inculcation of these habits boosts immune function, improves emotional intelligence, reduces stress, controls irritation and aggression, reduces blood pressure, heart risk, and cancer. Even if you don't have the dire need for any of it, it still makes sense to meditate and exercise regularly as it improves your focus and concentration. And it's one thing which can never be substituted by any other success attribute. It's an inevitable requisite for success for which only you are responsible. And few of the ways you can get more focused are by practicing meditation, mindfulness, and daily exercise.

Action Challenge: *Practice mindfulness. In simple words it means paying attention to what you are thinking, becoming aware of your emotions like anger, sadness, excitement, being present while eating, bathing, walking, etc.*

CHAPTER SEVENTEEN

WEEKENDS ARE MEANT FOR FUN

Japan is famous for its work ethics and is infamous for "Karoshi"- a term used to describe "death from overwork." Yes, people there die of heart attacks and strokes due to overwork. Couldn't they have simply laid off? Is that what you are thinking? Well, even the thought of a sabbatical is met with chagrin by the Japanese. A survey conducted by Expedia shows that sixty-three percent of the Japanese feel guilty about taking paid leaves.[17.1] One reason being, people who take leaves have to deal with their condescending colleagues.

Their culture fosters workaholism. Japanese managers have been ranked as one of the least likely to approve leave. Having realized the magnitude of this problem, their government passed the Work Style Reform bill in 2018. They made it mandatory to take five days of vacation in a year. They even had to go to the extent of making it compulsory to allow a minimum interval between the end of day's work time and the next day's start time. They limited overtime work to forty five hours in a month in general and to a maximum of hundred hours a month in case of special agreements.

If you think a reform like this would have reduced Japan's output, you are utterly wrong. These reforms are presumed to increase Japan's productivity. As per a survey conducted in 2017, Japan ranks as the least productive nation among G7. However, in 2019, after the passing of reform, Japan surpassed France and Italy. Perhaps, the work style reform did work in its favor.

However, it's not only Japan that has been following a strict work regime. People from other parts of the globe are also reluctant to take a vacation to avoid being seen as a chair warmer. Those who take it, try to curtail it due to the feeling of an impending disrespect at work. Some refuse vacations because they haven't realized the amplitude of its benefits, and never did anyone bring it to their notice. Whatever the reason may be, Karoshi and Japan's productivity rankings make it clear that a monotonous elongated period of work does more harm than good to us. A short vacation in between the tedious routines can add much-needed flavors.

Taking a vacation can have both psychological and physical health benefits. People who go on holidays tend to have a better outlook on life and find a new inspiration to go back to their work. It improves not only their work-life but also their personal life. Those who spend quality time with their family on vacations are generally more satisfied in their lives and have an excellent work-life balance. A study even says that just by planning a vacation, one stays happy for about eight weeks before the holiday, in anticipation of it. Also, the scenic beauties of the places one visits induce fresh creativity in ways of doing things. Making an effort to try a new activity or going on a short hiking trip with the people you enjoy is a lot better than being a couch potato on a Sunday afternoon.

A study conducted by Stanford University states that "for most workers, weekly output rises with weekly hours of work, although, after a point, the increase in output declines as more hours are worked." Until forty-eight hours a week, weekly output responds proportionally to hours worked. However, as weekly hours surpass forty-eight hours, the marginal product declines. The proportionate increase in output becomes insensitive to the proportionate increase in the working hours beyond forty-eight hours of the workweek. The same study also implies that output is slightly higher on a forty-eight-hour work week (with no Sunday) than on a seven-day work schedule.[17.2]

In this technological era, the relation of output with input hasn't remained linear. With the emergence of technology and capital intensive industries, rarely any work is left entirely in the hands of human beings. Today, the critical job an employee does is thinking. Had our jobs required physical labor, we could have measured our productivity with the number of hours worked. But now, our job requires value addition while quantity is left for the machines. With these changes in demands of the time, the best output from a human being won't come with increasing hours but would come with efficient functioning.

Companies like Google, IKEA, General Motors, Ericsson-Worldwide, JP Morgan Chase & Co., Microsoft prioritize the workers' needs for a refreshing break and even encourage taking a vacation with the concept of paid leaves. On the other hand, Netflix, LinkedIn, Grub hub, and Twitter are well-known companies that offer unlimited paid time off to their employees. These companies encourage people to enjoy their life because they understand that happy people bring more to the table than lifeless souls.

It is interesting to note that as per the US travel association, fifty-five percent of the American employees have unused vacation time in 2018.[17.3] In the name of prioritizing our work, we are not only losing a cheerful personal life but also our productivity. Not using our vacation time for the sake of our work is counterproductive. Most of the employees check their work emails on vacation. Intending to build a strong work ethic, we are neither utilizing our breaks properly nor making progress in our work. We cannot do justice to work without taking sufficient time off. The world's topmost elite performers make sure they take adequate breaks in between their training periods. Rest periods are part of their training. Their coaches know the human body cannot function optimally without giving sufficient recovery time.

Usain Bolt, an eight-time Olympic champion, takes four to eight weeks off every year from his training. The same is true for David Rudisha and Mo Farah, who take six to twelve weeks and four weeks off, respectively.[17.4] Mo Farah's coach Alberto Salazar in an interview, says, "We work on two twenty-week cycles, so that's forty weeks. You ask, where are the other twelve weeks? After each 20-week cycle, we have a two-week period, which is basically off, usually two weeks of no running whatsoever, and then we have two weeks of jogging. So that's four weeks of recovery after each cycle, and then we have another two weeks of moderate build-up training, and then we are back into the heavy training." Whether it's an Olympic champion or a software engineer, we all need good breaks to maintain our willingness and motivation levels. Coming back from a vacation or a short holiday quickly fills us with instant motivation for work. The zeal we get naturally after a time off is incomparable.

To showcase your work ethic, take time off. And while doing that, don't fuss over your work. Enjoy your weekends to the fullest. Don't let your office tensions get to you. Don't let it wreck your joy. Enjoy every moment of it. Train your brain to give your undivided attention to whatever you do. Remind yourself how deeply you had submerged in your work after returning from your last trip? If you didn't, don't find fault with the vacation. The problem could be with your work. You could be pushing yourself into something that you don't love because those who love their work rejoice it at any hour of the day.

Action Challenge: *Notice your enthusiasm at work each day. Find out when do you feel most motivated? Is it after a break (say Monday) or before a break (say Friday)?*

CHAPTER EIGHTEEN

DECISION FATIGUE

How much of human error is admissible in judicial decisions? How many lives is it okay to stake due to our inability to make a correct decision?

There is a limit to our cognitive abilities. Not every decision can be right. Nor is our brain designed to take correct decisions. This became evident when Jonathan Levav conducted a study on the likelihood of rendering a favorable decision for granting parole. Irrespective of the cases' characteristics, judges were found to grant higher parole at the beginning of the workday than in subsequent sessions. The percentage of favorable outcomes gradually reduced from approximately sixty-five percent to near zero as the day passed, increasing abruptly after lunch to about sixty-five percent and thereby decreasing again.[18.1]

The chance of getting parole decreased as the day passed. Though it increased further after lunch breaks, as the judges took more decisions, it depleted again. Implying, irrespective of the case's details, a prisoner's chance to receive parole is higher when it is heard first. His life depends more on the number of cases the judge has heard before him than the facts. Making similar decisions throughout the day depletes our mental energy, reducing the chances of making the right decisions. The judges, being unaware of their mental fatigue, kept giving life-staking decisions to prisoners thinking their decision was rational when, in fact, it was influenced by the hour of the day.

With the increase in choices, the number of decisions we make daily has expanded. Our intuition may say choosing a restaurant is easy, but in contrast, we find ourselves beating our head while deciding a perfect restaurant for a casual dinner. Choosing an ice cream flavor or deciding what to wear seems simple. Still, we spend an unjustifiable amount of time making these minor decisions depleting our mental energy.

Most of us are unaware of the cognitive fatigue we face, but we do show its presence by getting irritated in the later hours. We think superficially while making decisions after a point and feel like getting rid of taking more decisions at the end of the day. That's one reason why Mark Zuckerberg, Steve Jobs, and Barack Obama wear similar outfits every day. They believe that each decision requires a certain amount of energy, and there's a limit to the maximum number of correct decisions one can make in a day. And they prefer to spend those decisions on improving their product rather than on deciding what to wear.

Decision fatigue is another reason why there has been much praise for minimalistic lifestyles recently. People have shifted towards having less and are finding their life turning much more peaceful and relaxing. Before 2019, I spent a minimum of five minutes every day gazing at my cupboard, deciding what to wear. It was a frustrating act. Imagine spending two and a half hours a month thinking which dress would look good on you for that specific day. The clothes weren't gifted, I bought them. I knew it would look good on me. Yet it took me time. Gladly after years of hustling, I came across a Netflix documentary on Minimalism that changed my perspective. I previously thought having more would make humans happier. But it made me realize the opposite. I realized, we feel happier when we release our mind of unnecessary everyday tension. We are calmer when we are off the silly competition. I instantly decided on ways to spend the least amount of time getting ready. I kept my clothes handly. I bought simple yet elegant dresses that can be worn at most places. I deliberately decided to wear a single formal attire for my youtube channel. That way, I released a significant burden from my mind. Imagine the pressure I would have gone through had I not taken this decision. How much time would it have taken? From buying clothes to deciding what to wear to pairing them up, I skipped a cumbersome process. I invested the same energy in writing beautiful content and inspiring youth through my channel. I also reduced the visual clutter I had in my room.

The issue with decision fatigue is that you are never really aware that you are tired of making decisions. You simply make poor decisions forgetting the consequences. The fast advent of technology has also made it much clear that coming to a decision is more important than coming to the right decision. If you are taking too much time to decide on trivial matters, you are wasting your energy. In the case of business decisions, if you are too slow in deciding, consider it less effective already. Jeff Bezos says,

"Most decisions should probably be made with somewhere around seventy percent of the information you wish you had. If you wait for ninety percent, in most cases, you're probably being slow. Plus, either way, you need to be good at quickly recognizing and correcting bad decisions. If you're good at course correcting, being wrong may be less costly than you think, whereas being slow is going to be expensive for sure".

Whether you want to be fast or you want to save your mental power, these days, it's wiser to adjust with okayish choices than to waste your willpower in making the best decisions. The American psychologist and the author of The Paradox of Choice, Barry Schwartz, explains the first step to make better decisions is to move from the mindset of always making the best decisions to making good enough decisions.

But why do we struggle to make decisions? Yes, we do have infinite choices, but didn't we want that? Having too many choices is not a problem. Fearing what we might miss is the reason why everybody is trying to find the best option. This fear is so much ingrained in us that it led to the coining of a new term, "FOBO- Fear of Better Options" by Patrick McGinnis. He explains FOBO keeps us from committing to choices that are well accepted due to the fear of what we might miss in the future, making us more dissatisfied and anxious. Nowadays, we have started to care less about being happy with achieving what we always wanted and worry more about what was never on our list of goals. Until we break this thinking pattern, we will keep trying to find better options for everything that catches our eyes.

Stop optimizing on little things. Optimizing while buying a house seems fair but while choosing a restaurant is unnecessary. Researchers say that people who try to optimize all the time are less happy than those who settle with "just fine" options. A study conducted by the University of Columbia found that graduates who tried to maximize the opportunity and accepted the job with a higher salary were less satisfied in the end than those who secured a job with lower salaries. Despite making better decisions and earning twenty percent higher salaries, the maximizers were unfulfilled compared to the satisfiers.[18.2]

Making decisions consumes a lot of time and energy. Those who have a habit of time tracking know how many significant hours they have wasted in ordering food. While I was living alone, I almost wasted thirty minutes daily deciding what to order. I was constantly trying to weigh the happiness I would have gotten by eating those dishes. Soon I realized this pattern and decided to settle with the "not so perfect options" or say the "good enough" options. I understood there is no end to finding the best food, nor is there an end to finding the best dress or the best show. While buying home appliances, I rarely take part in discussions just to save my energy and cognitive faculties. After all, a little less functionality in a refrigerator or washing machine would not affect me. An extra feature could always be a bonus! If an HD TV can let me see my favorite series on Netflix, it's good enough for me. The same goes for furniture, clothes, crockeries, etc. Until it has a direct impact on me, I even avoid taking part in discussions.

The depletion of mental abilities is hard to catch. Right decisions can make or break things. The number of decisions we make will keep rising. Amidst these scenarios, settling for a "just fine option" is the only way we have to make the best use of our minds. After all, who would like to compromise on the ability to launch a better product for choosing a tastier breakfast, and who would prefer to mess on making better career decisions for finding the best series to binge-watch! Let's accept our brain's limitations and act accordingly.

Action Challenge: For the next three days, count the number of minutes you spend making decisions. Notice the exhaustion you feel after making even a tiny decision like choosing a restaurant.

CHAPTER NINETEEN

SLEEP: IT MATTERS MORE THAN YOU THINK

How nice it would be if we could eliminate sleep! We would have got eight more hours each day to catch up on missing parts of life. Who doesn't want that? Probably that's the reason why we have successfully convinced ourselves to sleep less. Interestingly, it hasn't reduced our productivity. At least that's what we'd like to think. Thanks to caffeine! Our all-time savior. Though there is a lot of research both praising and defaming caffeine, one thing is worth noting- the molecular structure of caffeine is similar to adenosine, a compound whose absence initiates sleep. Adenosine is released by breaking down compounds from glucose. We feel sleepy when our body is deprived of it. Caffeine, having a similar molecular structure, replaces adenosine and fools our brain to stay awake. Even when we are tired, caffeine makes our body think it has enough energy resources to keep going.

When I was in college, one of my professors said, "It's just a matter of a few years of hard work, and then you will land into your dream jobs. Work hard for some time. Sleep less if need be". Listening to him, one student said, "I don't want to die early." Those days, the fact of dying early due to sleep deprivation was famous. The professor replied, "What will you do with those extra years of your life if you would be nothing?" Those words got stuck in my mind. I started sleeping less for around five hours a day. I was motivated to do the hard work. But didn't know it would have its consequences. Though I spent more wakeful hours, I doubt I was ever awake. I felt sleepy "all the time"! It took me way more time to learn new information compared to what it takes me today. I thought I was born with lousy concentration levels but never doubted my lifestyle choices. I relied on caffeine to keep myself awake, which had other ill effects. I suddenly noticed an upsurge in my stress levels. I generally loved exams. But this was the first time I was feeling too nervous, sometimes even to the extent of not being able to sleep for a whole night.

It took me a while to understand that my stress level had more to do with caffeine and less to do with exams. Soon I reduced my caffeine consumption, and the stress went away. However, understanding the importance of sleep was beyond my capacity at that time. Hard work was all over my mind. Though I was studying for more hours, the results weren't good. It took me some more years to finally realize the mistake I made, and since then, I have stopped compromising on my sleep. Now, I take pride in sleeping more.

Sleep has a vital role in rejuvenating our bodies. Human beings cannot function optimally without getting their cells repaired in time! Though we like to believe sleeping an hour less wouldn't affect us, research has shown staying awake for more than sixteen hours impairs waking neurobehavioral functions. Sleeping for less than six hours every night reduces cognitive performance equivalent to two nights of complete sleep deprivation. It's effect on our performance does not just last for a few moments but can be felt throughout the day.[19.1]

If you are one bloodthirsty vampire, then you don't need sleep. If you are a mortal like most others, sleep is the only way to keep you going. You don't have that 'humanity switch' to spare you the real-life melodrama. But you can indeed sleep it off. Sleep benefits need no validation, nor is there a consensus among the experts about the number of hours one should sleep except that sleep is necessary and that sleep quality is coal-and-ice.

As per the American Sleep Association, an estimated sixty million US citizens suffer from a sleep disorder. Over four percent of Americans aged twenty or more reported using prescription sleep aids in a particular month. Doesn't it sound weird that people are having problems sleeping? Isn't it one of the most natural things a body does? Since the inception of the twenty-first century, there has been a steep soar in sleeping pills sales like never before. There can be only one thing to blame for all of this- Poor Lifestyle Choices, resulting in sleep disorders impacting sleep quality. With the so-called rapid development of this twenty-first century, people started pushing their limits even in aspects which demand normalcy. Long working hours, late-night parties, excessive food intakes, high alcohol consumption, the whole cluster is responsible for the blistering attack on sleep. Further exacerbating the situation, reduced duration and lower sleep quality induce other health disorders like depression, anxiety, fatigue, and narcolepsy. With all this ravaging you, not just your work life, even your personal life is at stake. When stuck in this nexus, sleeping pills seem like a desperate measure to zonk out.

Sleeping pills, like every quick fix, come with a catch. Any drug without side effects is too good to be true. A sleeping pill is no exception. Irrespective of whether it is an over-the-counter or a prescription drug, the after-effects have convinced the FDA to order the use of strong warning labels. But, did you ever take it seriously? Keeping aside the general side effects like daytime drowsiness, dizziness, unusual dreams, and memory loss, there have been other adverse effects reported, such as the increased risk of accidents, depression with suicidal tendencies, higher risk of Alzheimer's and cancer.

Sleep is a vital element of our body's restoration process. It is indispensable to keep our human faculties in their ideal state without giving it a chance to convert short-term memory into long-term memory and repair cells. When we sleep, our body produces its muscle-building hormones, including Human Growth Hormone (HGH). An inadequate sleep, besides making us cranky, disrupts our cognitive abilities and their optimal functioning. It makes us more prone to anxiety & depression and more susceptible to cardiovascular diseases & diabetes. At the developing stage, a lack of sleep results in a short attention span, reduced reflexes, poor decision-making, weak memory, and in some cases, retarded physical growth.

Most people think when we sleep, our brain also goes into sleep mode. That's not true. The activity level in our brain rises when we are asleep. It increases further when we sleep after learning new information. One of our brain's significant activities during sleep is making newer connections from the information it has accumulated throughout the day. It repeats the neural activity performed by our brain when we were awake and makes us experience similar movements in the cortex and hippocampus during slow-wave sleep.[19.2]

Anyone who is aware of the role sleep plays would know the significance the next day's sleep has in memorizing recent data. That's one reason why researchers always tell students to sleep well before exams rather than wasting their time trying to mug up only to forget it sooner. But did you know that a full night's sleep after learning isn't the only factor responsible for your retention? Quality sleep a day before matters equally! To prove the point, Matt Walker, a professor of Neuroscience and Psychology, divided the participants into two groups. One group had a good night's sleep, and the other stayed awake under vigilance. The next day, all the participants learned a list of new facts while placed under an MRI scanner. Before the test and after learning the new information, they were asked to take two nights of proper sleep. Results showed that the group that did not sleep before the day of learning new facts learned forty percent less information than the group that slept well a day before. That happened because of hippocampus activity level, a part of the brain responsible for learning and retaining memories. The hippocampus of the sleep group showed lots of healthy learning-related activity, unlike the sleep-deprived group.[19.3] Many researchers believe we are still at the beginning of understanding the greatness of sleep. There hasn't been enough research done on this area to understand it entirely, but one thing the researchers have made clear is its vitality.

Would you agree if someone tells you we are more prone to get insights while sleeping than when we are completely awake and seriously trying to find the solution? Hard to believe, but that is precisely the truth. During sleep, our brain consolidates memory and builds up new neural connections. It goes through the same neural representation it went through the previous day during wakefulness. It digs into every bit and piece and leaves us with better insights when we wake up.

To prove the point, researchers divided the subjects into two groups. They gave them a set of cognitive tasks divided in ten parts. It also had a hidden trick. The subjects were to try the first three blocks to induce mental representation, followed by an interval. One group slept for eight hours during the interval while the other stayed awake. Later, when both the groups performed the complete set of tasks, the group that slept for eight hours gained double the insights than those who remained awake. The reason being, when we sleep, our brain goes through all the information it has captured. It goes through the details and makes newer connections. If you are doing hours of wakeful thinking, you are utterly underutilizing your free source of insights during sleep. Next time when you want to find a solution, sleep on it. Your chance of getting an intuition almost doubles in your sleep! [19.4]

Your productivity is a direct corollary of your energy levels, mood, alertness, and cognitive faculties. A good quality sleep ensures that all such needs are best met. Hence, it is recommended to do whatever it takes to improve your sleep quality to fully ensure that the restorative effects of sleep occur. Having peaceful surroundings, sleeping in isolation, switching off the electronic items, placing an ambient white noise, not sleeping on an empty stomach, staying hydrated, etc., ensures your body gets rested well. Practicing a relaxing ritual like sleep hypnosis and sleep meditation, avoidance of alcohol and caffeine, sticking to your sleep schedules even on holidays, and eating a healthy, nutrient-rich diet can help you sleep better. If the quality of sleep is not right, then the quantity cannot fill the void.

Interestingly, your sleep quality isn't the only factor that matters for your days to unfold well. How you wake up also has an effect. Those days when you wake up naturally on your own without the intervention of an alarm, you start your day with good vibes. In contrast, on the days when you wake up to your jarring alarm, you have a groggy start. It's not a mere coincidence. There's a reason behind this. An average person has four to five sleep cycles every night. One sleep cycle lasts approximately ninety minutes. If your alarm happens to ring precisely at the end of your sleep cycle, you will wake up at once without any inner resistance. But if it blares in the middle of a sleep cycle, you would probably snooze it and doze off back again. Even if you wake up, this abrupt start will have its impact throughout the day. It's also interesting to note that when you nestle back in your cozy bed after turning off your alarm, you presumably wake up around ninety minutes later, which is another sleep cycle, provided that your alarm doesn't yank you awake. After all, that's where the 'snooze' button steps in to save you from missing your morning meeting. It cannot help but disturb your sleep cycles. Not to worry, these days, we have alarm clocks that observe our sleeping pattern by detecting our movements and help us wake up at the end of our sleep cycles. It's called artificial 'intelligence' for a reason. Don't you think?

Here are some tips and tricks to help you slip into slumber faster- Reduce the activity as it gets dark. The action makes you alert and wards off your sleep. Keep your enthusiasm in check. It's not the right time to make things energetic. Reduce room temperature. Our body needs to lower its temperature to initiate sleep. Develop the habit of reading a book lying down in your bed until you fall asleep. If reading isn't your type, play an audiobook or a podcast that you find boring and concentrate on it with your eyes closed to keep your mind off any unsettling thoughts. You can also try sleep meditation, guided or silent. Set the timer so you don't have to look at your digital screen to switch it off while falling asleep. Chamomile tea is a safer counterpart of sleeping pills. You can have it thirty minutes before your sleep time to induce sleep. If nothing works, here's a disregarded golden tip- Work hard throughout the day. Even your worst nightmares would fail to keep you awake.

Action Challenge: For the next ten days sleep for a minimum of eight hours. On the eleventh day, deliberately sleep for six hours and notice the difference you feel mentally and physically.

FOCUS

CHAPTER TWENTY

YOU CAN'T EXCEL AT EVERYTHING AT ONCE

You all would have passed by those gigantic, imposing mansions housed by the opulent families in those swanky areas. Have you ever wondered how life could be inside? Undoubtedly extravagant! But what about the happiness quotient? It would be wrong to think that all the affluent people lead a jubilant life. Fortunately, happiness, my friend, doesn't rely on wealth. Many people have reached great heights in their careers, made more money than they can ever spend, and built a circle filled with influential people. But at the end of the day, some aren't happy. With the paced up success-oriented outlook, it's happening too often lately. One can't say whom to blame! With so many examples out there, people have understood happiness has got nothing to do with riches. People have started to realize the importance of a balanced lifestyle. Broadly, a balanced life has six notable aspects:

Career - wealth, knowledge, respect, recognition, etc.

Personal - hobbies, interests, self-development, etc.

Relationship - with partner, childrens, parents, etc.

Social - friends, events, clubbing, etc.

Health - physical, mental and emotional wellbeing, food choices, etc.

Spiritual - meditation, yoga, prayer, affirmations, etc.

All of us consider these areas as significant aspects of happy living. Having said that, trying to excel in all the six spots at once is a recipe for disaster. At any given point in time, one should not think of mastering more than two aspects of life. Every now and then, the other sites will have to be set on the backburner. Depending on your age and responsibilities, you may choose any two aspects which need your maximum attention. Sometimes, to feed a particular area, you might have to starve the others. It makes complete sense to not fret about the meaning of god when you are planning to start your own business. Understanding this simple concept might help you avoid the moral dilemma. It can also unleash you from the guilt of underperforming in a less preferred area of your life. Every aspect of life has been assigned age and a juncture. Nobody devised it with an agenda, but it has gotten enrooted over time with the apprehension of the requirements. Here is a brief discussion on what shall deserve your attention at different points of time.

The order in which the six notable aspects of life have been arranged above is the order in which most people actualize these aspects in their lives. As you can see, spirituality has the backseat of all. Contrary to popular beliefs, spirituality deserves much attention at an early age. A well awakened, focused, peaceful, and stable mind can achieve higher success in real terms.

Many young people say they would start meditating in their 50's. They know its benefits, yet are determined to allocate time for it at the end of their lifespan. Don't you think if we are well aware that something is advantageous to us, we should be consuming it at the earliest? Spiritual awakening is a well-accepted notion for today's tech giants. When Mark Zuckerberg was having a hard time during initial Facebook days, his mentor Steve Jobs asked him to visit an Indian temple. He spent a month in the temple observing how people love to connect. Sitting there he realized how much better the world can become if everyone had a stronger ability to connect. That visit reinforced in him the business model he was working on and made him confident about his goals.

After spirituality, our personal self deserves attention. It's the site where we hatch the building blocks of our life. Until the late '20s, we are in the best phase for trying novel things, inculcating scrupulous habits, exploring our minds, and analyzing ourselves sincerely. These trials and errors get the best out of us and equip us with the wisdom to choose our path shrewdly at the crossroads of life. As the perfect formula cannot be formed by following what others say, it gets formulated with consistent experiments.

I once heard that the activities you loved to do in your early childhood days for fun are more likely to be discovered as your passion in later years. You could try listing down your favorite pastimes of childhood, and you will be surprised to learn that you still love to do some of the activities you have listed. These are the activities that have more chances of becoming your passion down the line. If you find it hard to remember, take help from your parents. They are the ones you can rely on for such information.

The '20s are the period of your life when you can focus on yourself. It's the time when you are devoid of the forthcoming responsibilities. You are mature enough to understand your calling, your likings, and dislikings by this time. Warren Buffet says, "By far, the best investment you can make is in yourself." When you are in your 20's, it's imperative to invest in yourself. By the end of it, all you will be left with is time to practice and hone your skills.

The third significant aspect of a balanced life is to have a flourishing career. Notably, we spend more than one-third of our life working. Who wants to impoverish such a massive period of work that doesn't please them? Reminds me of what Ray Bradbury said: "Love what you do and do what you love." What we need is not just to work but to find work that we think deserves thirty-three percent of our life span. A work that we think is worthy enough to spend our life on and an area we can excel at. While I was having a hard time deciding on my career choice, my friend gave me this billion-dollar advice. He said, "There's less than 0.0000000001% chance of you being born as a human; why waste it on doing something you don't like". This life-altering advice brought a metamorphic change in my life. It made me rethink everything I was doing, everything I was caught in, and everything society embedded in me as a goal.

Next comes your relations. Even when everything seems perfect, the absence of the right partner can make you feel like something is missing. Napoleon Hill, the author of the widely famous success book "Think and Grow Rich," explains that the combination of emotions of sex, love, and romance is capable of turning a man into a genius. Sex, being the most potent human desire; when it doesn't get its outlet through physical means, it connects the person to a higher power. When that energy combined with love gets invested in a particular work, the genius in the person takes birth. It is then the success of a person becomes inevitable.

Humans are emotional beings with the need for cohabitation. The purpose of families is to maintain the well being of its members. It is a place of intimacy, love, and trust that the early humans needed to protect their tribe from the outside dangers. This communion has been more of a necessity than a choice. Most people in their 40's aren't generally happy being alone. They yearn for their spouse, kids, or parents, and if they are not fortunate enough, they look for an external source of happiness. No matter what, this need for relations does not vanish unless one transfigures into a monk. When it's so evident that the need would arise anyway, why not make a deliberate effort to solve it beforehand?

Next is the social circle. Japan is the only country with seventy thousand centenarians. That's because Japanese people have a very strong healthy social life. Social circle plays a significant role when we are in the autumn of our life. Once we have fulfilled our responsibilities, social engagements breathe a new life into us. When we get old, all we need is someone to talk to, affectionate to us, and understand us. There is considerable evidence that proves that the stronger and happier you are through your social circle, the longer you live.

Though the last, never to be ignored, is your health. This is one such exceptional aspect of life that can never be left to the mercy of others. If you are not in the pink of your health, then it's a chink in your armor. When you are not in your best form, mentally or physically, nothing goes right for you. Life ends up in the soup when we let our health slip away. However, the way we have brought various complexities in our food, environment, and diseases, it has become inevitable to ignore health entirely in the first place. Being mindful about your choices and observing your body's needs can help you avoid early health problems.

The above hierarchy is merely a thought about what shall occupy our attention at different stages of life. It's a contemplation of when what shall be given more care and attention. There are no hard and fast rules for better living. There can only be good directives. We need not stick to the plan, we may shuffle our priorities as per our needs, but we must try to be prudent in our decision. Alas, being humans, we tend to digress from our resolute path as nothing in life goes as we plan it. Still, it's the equilibrium between these aspects that makes our life so beautiful. All I mean to say is that we should be more mindful of our choices. We shouldn't force ourselves to be good at everything. Unnecessary and impractical goals and responsibilities will burn us out before we have achieved anything in life. Take a minute and look where you are standing and assess what's right for you to do now. Focus on any two aspects of your choice at one time and try to manage the rest somewhat.

When I was struggling with my career, my good friend and a remarkable career counselor explained this concept. He said, "You are doing amazingly well with your relationship and social circle. You are successful in what you are focusing on. If you shift your focus, you would be successful in other areas too. You can be good at whatever you do just if you focus your energy".

That insight got me engrossed in myself. I realized that when I am not doing well, it means that I am not aligning myself. That one thought altered the outlook I had about myself. I was doing great in the area I was putting my energy on and wasn't prospering in the areas I ignored. He also shared that when he was building his career, he had to give up on many fun and social activities that others cherished. Relationship and spiritual activities barely crossed his mind back then. Though he always managed the other areas fairly, he never tried to excel in them. He didn't make the mistake of judging himself on something that was never his goal.

For people these days, life is full of hiccups. Our delirious standpoint, which promotes an incoherent viewpoint, is to be blamed. We rate ourselves on something which was never our ambition. We wish for something which was never our dream in the first place. We fight the battles which were never meant to be fought. Our concepts of success have become wacky. In short, we are not clear of our priorities, and even if we are, we want to see ourselves as the masters of everything. As a result, our relationships take a toll when it's time to take our careers seriously. Our detrimental lifestyle poses inadvertent health issues at an early age. Fierce career competition begins even before our subconscious is fully developed. We rarely find our spiritual calling. Spirituality is mostly a forced upbringing to us. And with all of it wreaking havoc on our psychological wellbeing, our conscience is impaired to such an extent that we are unable to make laudable decisions.

Keep yourself focused. Take only two aspects of life to take care of at the moment and let the rest wait till you set up what the time demands. Meanwhile, do not carry the burden to excel in everything. Give enough time to the endeavors that are of grave importance to you at the moment. Do not judge yourself for underperforming in the other areas. As Johann Wolfgang Von says, "Things which matter most must never be at the mercy of things which matter least." Find the thing that matters to you now and forget the rest.

Action Challenge: Encircle two aspects that are imperative for you at the current phase of your life. Work dedicatedly on them for no less than a year while fairly managing the rest.

Spiritual
Personal
Career
Relationship

Social
Health

YOUR FOCUS DETERMINES YOUR REALITY

"We always overestimate the change that will occur in the next two years and underestimate the change that will occur in the next ten. Don't let yourself be lulled into inaction".

-Bill Gates

We all are different. We all have different physical and intellectual capabilities. We all have different interests. But can two people having similar physical and intellectual strengths win the same battle? Remember, we don't have just one Olympic winner; we have a new winner every year. We have many great footballers, cricketers, boxers, writers, actors, scientists, dancers, singers, and entrepreneurs. By virtue of a race, we have a winner. But that does not conclude that one who comes second or trails last can never capture the throne.

Anyone can be great in the area of their choice. Anyone can become the next Picasso. But what should an average person do to attain that level of mastery? How can an average person become an expert? Is it just practice, or can we say people are born with talent? Through his research paper "The Role of Deliberate Practice," famous psychologist Anders Ericsson argues that expert performance is not based on innate talent but is rather a result of continuous practice.

For a long time, people argued about the role of genetics in performance. Whether it's the height of a basketball player or the speed of neural transmission, we have believed people's genetics have helped them attain their successes. However, researchers have found no more than a 0.2 correlation between mental ability and occupational success. Nor is there any significant correlation between height/weight/size of muscle and sports performance. Though they have acted as an added advantage, they can not be stated as the reason for attaining mastery.

Various researchers have found that experts have been able to produce their best works only after turning 34. To be precise, 35.4 in the case of scientists and 34.3 in poets and authors. Though the average age at which they produced their first work was ten years earlier, 25.2 in the case of scientists and 24.2 in poets and authors, they could not create their best ones until ten years of deliberate practice. And let's not forget they started practicing much before they produced their first work.[21.1] Whether it's the case of producing music, making a new scientific discovery, or playing a mastermind game like chess, rarely has anyone attained status as a master before ten years of deliberate practice.

An average person typically sees a talented man as a gifted child. However, a series of research has proved that mastery can be achieved by all with practice, and innate talent is limited to very basic characteristics contributing in its lowest form compared to meticulous practice. This means anyone can become an expert performer even without natural talent if he hones the required skill. Talent is innate, but skill could be mastered. Victory need not always be tamed by the talented; it can also be enslaved by the skilled.

"I believe the true road to preeminent success in any line is to make yourself master IN THAT LINE. I have no faith in the policy of scattering one's resources, and in my experience, I have rarely if ever met a man who achieved pre-eminence in money-making... certainly never one in manufacturing.. who was interested in many concerns. The men who have succeeded are the men who have chosen one line and stuck to it."

Andrew Carnegie

Great results require persistent practice and focus. One can't do all and shall not try it either. The ability to focus is rare. Not everyone can dare to choose a thing and spend their life on it. It's the rarest of the times when somebody gathers the courage to follow a specific path. With that, I want to ask you, when was the last time you sole heartedly worked on a particular thing for more than a few months without letting your focus get diverted into anything apart from the work you have chosen? When was the time when you didn't care about anything else but only about the work you had taken up?

Becoming great requires focus. And we all trade very loosely with this fact. Very few of us take up something and work devotedly until it's done. Forget about the months. We can't even keep ourselves focused on one thing for a day. On a typical day, most of us get our hands dipped into many things. We rarely give significance to focusing on one thing and get into anything and everything that catches our attention. We choose the task on a first-come, first-serve basis and do not put effort into choosing them deliberately.

To stay on track, you must continuously discern what is crucial to you at the moment. It could be a project you are working on or a startup idea or an exam, or maybe your health. But once you are sure of the work you want to do, do not look at anything else.

When Arne Sorenson, the CEO of Marriott International, was asked the secret behind Marriott's success, he attributed it to two things- care for people and focus. He said, "We had a period when we were sort of a mini conglomerate, we were in timeshare and senior living and cruise ships and several other things, but increasingly in the last thirty years, it's been focus-focus-focus on the hotel business.[21.2]

I recently visited a friend's place during a festival, and the walls adorned with exquisite handmade artworks grabbed my attention. I wondered why women at his home were more creative than the ones at my house. Later, I realized that in his family, women spend most of their time at home doing various chores due to their cultural background and a different set of norms and beliefs. These women were deprived of education and lifestyles that are followed by women in other parts of the world. As a result, they got more time to spend on creative works. They got more time to hone their skills. Their confinement did more good than bad for their attention. They lived in their small beautiful world with lots of space and time to focus. And their steadfast focus had yielded staggering results.

When Mark Parker became CEO of Nike, he got a congratulatory call from Steve Jobs. Mark asked Jobs for his advice, and Jobs said, "Well, just one thing- Nike makes some of the best products in the world. Products that you lust after. Absolutely beautiful stunning products. But you also make a lot of crap. Just get rid of the crappy stuff and focus on the good stuff." Steve had stood by this mantra in Apple. When he was reinstated in Apple, the company was involved in too many products. After a few weeks he realized, they can't move ahead by trying to build everything. In a review meeting, he drew a box, divided it into four parts, and wrote "Consumer" and "Pro" above the columns and "Desktop" and "Portable" beside the rows. He then asked his employees to build one product for each quadrant. He canceled more than seventy percent of products the company was then working on, laid off three thousand employees, and turned the company into a $300 million profit from a loss of $1 billion. Before his arrival, the company was merely ninety days far from being insolvent.[21.3] He knew until they focused all their resources on a few products, they might come up with many fine products, but none of them would touch the heart of their users.

Peter Drucker once said, "There is nothing so useless as doing efficiently that which should not be done at all." We all know that ignoring what not to do is much more important than what to do to maintain our focus, but rarely do we stand true to our apprehension. All of us are guilty of this mistake, yet we follow this concept scarcely. We postpone the things that require focus, serving us the ultimate satisfaction, for not much in return. If we only could gather the courage to focus on the aspects that require the hour's need, we can move mountains. Your efforts have utility only when you focus on the right path. Even a considerable amount of hard work would not deliver the results you desire if you fail to focus. You could do okay, but not great.

Focus plays a pivotal role in success. But how do you learn to focus? To be able to focus well, you need to first figure out what deserves your attention and what has to be kept aside. The only way you can take this big decision is by having your facts right. Deciding upon something is not tough. Sticking to it is! You got to find something that's worth it and something that convinces you to avoid everything else. One way to smartly land on a tough decision is by listing down the pros and cons. Of course, we do it all the time, so what's new over here? This time we are not listing the pros and cons to decide, but we are listing them to see through what we are choosing. Because, whether we like it or not, there always comes a day when we doubt our decision, and the other options look attractive. However, when we choose our options, being well aware of their cons, the doubt in our mind vanishes sooner. To not get bewildered later, we shall accept the negatives beforehand. And once we are sure of our choices, all we need to do is "focus."

To understand how focus can bring a significant difference in your life, just for the next two weeks, decide to work on one specific project. Test it out. Set aside two weeks for a specific work. You may choose something as simple as learning marketing or full-fledged hiring or working on a new project. See for yourself the difference it brings in your results. I call this technique of working- focus weeks.

When we work for long uninterrupted periods, we transition to a phase where we start to act smoothly with minimal effort. We do the same amount of work without needing extra willpower and energy. Our thoughts become saturated, the inner dialogues stop, and our actions towards the task get automated. When we commit ourselves entirely to one job for a week or two, we develop the state of flow, which helps us glide through our work. Our subconscious comes into the picture and overtakes the work done by our conscious mind. It's precisely how we brush teeth, take showers, or drive cars. We don't use our cognitive mind for the activities where we have already trained our subconscious. When we make it a habit, our subconscious develops the skill and reduces the amount of effort otherwise required. The subconscious mind, which is much faster than the conscious mind, uses its natural speed and shuts off the work done by the conscious brain, and gets the job done faster with the least effort.

Focus weeks also work best for new ideas. Great ideas should never be left to the mercy of others. They deserve full attention. Yet, most of us fall short on trusting our ideas and stall in making decisions due to fear of failure. Any new work requires setting up the initial process, which seems like a project in itself. Yes, our work does require our time depending on its size, but once we are done with the initial process, things start to run smoothly, requiring less effort and attention. Whether it's setting up a new business or moving to a new city, it requires initial pain, and then everything looks plain and simple. Focus weeks help you set up the pace and lets you follow it easily later on. It gives you time to really think and work intensely on an idea and realize its potential. After all, you can always move back to your previous routine if you later find things not working your way.

A research by Cornell University states that in the end, most human beings regret what they could have done but had not, rather than what they should have done but did not. They do not regret not taking the responsibilities of life but rather lament the ideal state of achievement they wanted for themselves in which they did not act. Most of us focus on accomplishing the shoulds of life. We give our best shot in fulfilling our responsibilities. But when it comes to fulfilling our dreams, we play small. Though, when it comes it regretting, the shoulds carry no weight in comparison to our dreams. [21.4]

Last year when I came across a quick online business idea, I did not take action immediately. I felt I already have much on my plate, and I cannot ponder on anything extra. At the same time, I didn't want to let go of the idea. I wanted to try it out. Around five weeks passed, and by the end of every week, I realized I didn't do anything substantial and was only passing weeks with minimal work. Disappointed with my past performance, I decided to spend a whole week on that idea. I pleasantly surprised myself with the amount of work I finished in such a short period. Looking at my pace, I decided to extend my focus week for another week. I worked wholeheartedly, avoiding every other thing coming my way. I wondered if I could have ever accomplished that sort of work even after a month. I immediately felt guilty for wasting so many weeks of my life postponing to work on a great idea for almost nothing.

Many of us pay a high price by postponing to act on our ideas. The return we get is minimal compared to the cost we pay. If you are postponing something due to its size or the amount of effort it would require but are sure of getting good results, focus weeks can be your best resort.

Focus weeks work well in case of setting up an entirely new work system. Whether you have a new project or a new idea, setting aside two weeks wholly dedicated to it will surely change things for the better. Any big project that requires a long, continuous effort can benefit from this technique by seeking your complete dedication for a reasonable period. To make the most of it, prioritize the tasks you want to get done. Write down everything in detail and just go for it. Start from scratch and take baby steps, one at a time. Don't waste time thinking, and don't underestimate the amount of work you can finish by the end. Do not entertain any other ideas when you are on a focus week. Stick to the plan. I am sure you will surprise yourself with the volume of tasks you will get done in just two weeks.

Action Challenge: Choose an area of work for the next two weeks, which, if given complete attention, can change things favorably for you.

CHAPTER TWENTY-TWO

CHOOSE YOUR BATTLES

Cambridge Dictionary defines productivity as "the rate at which a person, company, or country does useful work." The words' Rate' and 'Useful' are worth giving special attention. As the speed with which you finish a task can alter your output, and the work you decide to do and not to do can amplify your results. It makes no sense to complete a task with high speed and efficiency that delivers zero output. If you see from a general perspective, many things would fit into the definition of the word 'useful.' However, if you decide a task's usefulness from the perspective of your goals, many of your choices would have to be replaced or eliminated.

We all have one specific dream very close to our hearts. It's like the ultimate goal of our life. Though we get into many other things, we still know that even if we become successful in those areas, it would not give us as much happiness as we would have got from achieving our ultimate goals. Many of us want to stand for the intolerance around us. We want to fight for the mistreatment we have received. We want to be liked by people. We want to teach others a lesson, and the list goes on. Our list ranges from the most beautiful things to the deadliest of the activities. Despite being well aware that these circumstantial activities drain us and, in the end, do not add much to our happiness quotient, we compulsively do them.

You have to understand that it isn't possible to fight for everything and win it all the time. Because, even if you are winning at something, you can be losing on something else. To fulfill your dreams, you have to miss out on winning smaller battles of life. You got to choose what deserves your time. Not everything is equally important. Not everything gives you equal happiness. You need to find the dream that's worth the fight. The diligent person inside us knows what is essential and what delivers results. However, this diligent person does not understand that, to do what we want to do, we need to first get rid of what we don't want to do. A few years back, I made the mistake of not choosing my battles. I was fighting back everything I was coming across until my father turned an exemplar of focus.

One day my parents quarreled, and my mother ended up being a picture of misery. It's never a soothing scene to watch your mother cry. It made me furious at my father. It started because my father chose to be a mute spectator in a situation that was slipping out of control. But there was a good chance for things to go south had he fought the issue. With a detached disposition, my father retired to his room soon after the row due to his sleep time at 11 p.m. But I remained agitated for much longer, which was why sleep was a distant reality. Halfway through the night, out of uncontrolled anguish, I marched into my father's room to let him know what I was going through. After earnestly listening to my side of the story, he taught me one of the biggest lessons of my life. He said, "You can't fight everything. You can't waste your energy on these frivolous matters. Such things will keep happening, but you are born for a bigger cause. If you spend all your energy on the trivial matters of life, you wouldn't be left with considerable energy to achieve your goals. You need to decide if this is the issue you want to spend your life on or you have a bigger problem to solve in this world". My anguish turned into realization in no time. I realized I was fighting over a trivial matter. I was surprised by the way I had overreacted to a petty issue. That lesson brought to my consciousness the amount of time and energy I had wasted previously by fiddling around. Since then, I have always engrossed myself only in battles that are worth my time. I firmly believe and assert that you should too!

Sometimes in life, we have to let go of things. None of us has the power to stop petty issues, quarrels, fights, problems from cropping up, but we do have the power to choose to fight or not to fight them. Not everything deserves equal attention. Not letting go of trivial matters only worsen our mood. It's better if we accept that a few things will always be out of our control. It can be anything ranging from a family matter to a squabble with friends or colleagues to a business argument. There will always be some people who will try to drag you into such issues, maybe because they don't have bigger goals and purpose in their lives, or they just don't know how to tackle their lives' problems. But remember, it's always your choice how far you get in. There's a great saying by George Bernard Shaw, "I learned long ago, never to wrestle with a pig. You get dirty, and besides, the pig likes it". Beware of such people who are sitting just to drain your energy with their evil motives. I know that I sound harsh and despairing. But it's life, and it's a world where both angels and devils live.

However, it's not always others who drag us into these pitfalls. Sometimes we make mistakes too. We keep getting our nose into a situation that has zero probability of success. Even though we know, we keep doing it. Sometimes because of the emotions attached to the amount of time we had invested or sometimes because we don't know, there's a way out. Let me give you a simple example. When you go shopping and spend a decent amount of time with the salesman, there's a high chance he would be willing to sell you a product for a lesser price by the end. Also, there's a good chance even if it's out of your budget, you would buy. You wouldn't buy it because you'll be more convinced about the product. You would buy it because of the time you had invested. Likewise, the salesman wouldn't sell because he finds it viable to reduce the price. He would sell it because of the effort and energy he had spent making that deal. The same applies to our personal and professional life as well. Many people don't want to continue their careers, but they do it because of the amount of time they have spent. People find it hard to come out of bad relations because of the time and emotions attached to the person.

In Sep 2020, Mumbai's Municipal Corporation demolished Kangana Ranaut's office, claiming that the structure violated the construction guidelines. The office, which seemingly followed the construction norms until the previous day, was termed illegal and was thus demolished.

Kangana Ranaut is a famous actress in India. She is outspoken and frivolous. Everyone knows that the demolition of her office had little to do with the design's fault but more to do with the arguments she was putting forth against the ruling state government.

Well, politics being politics, all one can say is "it happens." But the question that pops up is- did it help her? Did it change things for the better? Was the mental harassment worth the words she uttered and the voice she raised? Well, if her goal was to expose the internal politics, she perhaps made the right move. But I doubt it was about that. Had it been, she would have taken various other measures to solve India's societal issues. She could have taken a formal route, launched her movement against mishappenings, could have brought like-minded people together, and raised her voice against societal wrongs in a formal manner.

It is a sheer waste of time and energy for an actress to get into these issues. The amount of time she would spend on settling the court case against the politicians and building her new office could have been invested in a blockbuster movie and other progressive ideas, let alone the mental impact it had on her. Indeed, had the same amount of effort been invested through an organized manner on fighting the issue, it could have initiated a new movement in the country and would have created a higher impact in society.

Fighting different battles in life is not a problem, but it's always wise to be thoughtful of the battles you want to get in. Do not get into unnecessary troubles just for the sake of doing some things. Rather than frivolously throwing yourself in, choose your battles, plan your activities, and make lasting impacts.

To be sure you aren't wasting your precious time fighting the wrong battles, find out if you are acting out of urge or have logic for conducting the way you are conducting yourself. Check if you are fighting to satisfy yourself emotionally or you are fighting for the right cause. Until you develop the discipline of choosing the right battles every day, you will keep fighting with the same pig trying out your luck. You got to choose a battle that has more for you. You got to decide on a day-to-day basis. Every day you have to make trade-offs in your life. The more thoughtful the trade-off is, the better it is.

Action Challenge: *List down all the irrelevant battles you are fighting now and cease them from today itself. Take required actions.*

CHAPTER TWENTY-THREE

PRIORITIZE, NOT EVERYTHING IS IMPORTANT

Time, money, and energy are three things that are limited to everyone. When it comes to money, we take it seriously because we know we will have to face the repercussions if it goes meager. But, when it comes to time and energy, we don't comprehend its importance until it's too late. Money can be earned, energy can be regained, but lost time can never come back.

Time and energy aren't taken gravely by most people because there is no way to measure the damage caused by their loss. They are only respected by businessmen, who can calculate the hourly profits generated, or by the people who are wise enough to fathom the ramifications of taking them for granted. Everyone has got equal hours. How one manages it makes all the difference. On one side of the world, Richard Branson is controlling four hundred different businesses. On the other hand, a common man finds it too tough to finish his day's task well.

Most people think time management is about micromanaging. Though some people might succeed in micromanaging their time occasionally, that's not how it works. Time management is less about micromanaging and more about moving forward with the right mentality and the right choices. If your mindset and choices aren't appropriately aligned, whatever technique you may use for time management would fall apart. On some days, you would lack motivation and dedication. Sometimes, you would be caught by your emotions. On other days, you might not be doing things the right way. Minor distractions or the speed of your internet connection are enough to ruin your productive drive.

When you are aiming for something, it's not just about what you decide to do. It's also about ignoring the insignificant activities and utilizing all your time and energy on what is worthy of taking you to your goal. Many people rely on 'to-do lists' to have clarity of tasks they need to accomplish. However, to-do lists are designed in such a way that it gives you the instant gratification of visually ticking off the completed tasks. Sadly, most of the time, they merely give you the illusion that things are getting done.

Though it's ok to depend on a checklist once in a while to finish various minute tasks, say while going grocery shopping or packing for a trip, it isn't an idea to use daily. In ventures where a high level of safety measures are required, like flying an airplane or procedures to be done before surgery, to-do lists unquestionably saves the doers from making mistakes. But in everyday life, most of us are not required to finish so many activities. But indeed are needed to complete one specific task that can make a difference. Checking off things in a to-do list does indicate a higher output. However, productivity isn't about the number of jobs you finish. It's about tackling the tasks that provide the most results/output without increasing your efforts/ input.

Rather than having a long to-do list, set daily/weekly priorities. Include two critical targets as per your priorities that need to be achieved by the end of the day. That way, you won't find yourself racing against time to check-off your list instead of doing the work. Every week set one or two priorities aligned with your short-term goals. Remember, one is always better than two. However, if you have two priorities, divide the day into two parts and allocate strict timings for each priority, say 8 AM to 2 PM for priority one and 2 PM to 7 PM for priority two. Try not to mix them. When you allocate your priorities to a specific time, your brain starts working like an alarm clock. It triggers your mind when the time comes, exactly how it makes you have lunch on time, even when you are not hungry.

Deciding on priorities is tough, especially when you have to choose one out of many. The best way to tackle such a situation is by using the 'why power.' Write down all the things you want to do and the 'why' behind doing them. Think of the significant activities that consume your time and let your mind pitch for them. Keep thinking of the pros and cons until you find something specific that deserves your attention.

This technique will help you set up your days without distraction and will let you focus on your priorities rather than the ancillaries like constant appointments, meetings, and invitations. It sets a clear path for your brain by helping you deny everything else that comes your way. If needed, dedicate a day every week to complete other unavoidable tasks. Prioritizing works better when your priorities are a subset of your yearly goals. A goal itself requires the completion of several activities. Your weekly priority shall be one of the core activities you need to do to accomplish your final goal.

Adam Grant, professor of psychology, says, "There are a limited number of hours in the day, and focusing on time management just makes us more aware of how many of those hours we waste. A better option is attention management: Prioritize the people and projects that matter, and it won't matter how long anything takes".[23.1]

Adam Grant, professor of psychology, says, "There are a limited number of hours in the day, and focusing on time management just makes us more aware of how many of those hours we waste. A better option is attention management: Prioritize the people and projects that matter, and it won't matter how long anything takes".[23.1]

Steve Jobs says, "Deciding what not to do is as important as deciding what to do." But how do you not do what you need to do? How do you prioritize when you have so many things on your plate? There's only one way out: by delegating effectively. You can't prioritize until you practice delegation. We all are guilty of biting off more than we can chew. We think of doing all the tasks ourselves either because we think we can do it better or because we forget we can delegate them. You may find yourself labeling some tasks as too trivial to delegate or may find it easier to do it yourself than teach others the intricacies. Sometimes, it's also a question of image and being too shy to ask for help. If you suffer from nondelegation, you are not alone. Many people, who even after so many years of experience and knowing well of its benefits, still aren't comfortable delegating.

To not let yourself get distracted by the amount of work you need to do and keep yourself focused on the goal, you must stop trying to do everything yourself. It's far better to focus your concentration on the crucial tasks than managing the trivial matters. To do that, follow these steps of delegation:

Step 1. Make a list of all the activities you do on a daily basis. Skip the one-time tasks and focus on those tasks which get repeated daily.

Step 2. Define these task on a broader aspect and divide them into the following four categories:

A - Activities that are either a core part of your work or require your core skills. These are the activities you think only you can do well. Your skill and experience lie here. This is what you are best at.

B - Crucial tasks that can not be avoided but can be done by others. Be it your family members or your team members. The important part is that someone is there who can do it well.

C - Managerial tasks: These are the tasks that require your management and leadership skills. These aren't your core activities, but you have to do it whether you like it or not. This category mostly involves managing, leading, overseeing, decision making, etc.

D - Tasks that are not crucial; can be avoided and can easily be taken care of by others.

You can think of the 80/20 rule to distinguish between your core and non-core activities. The famous 80/20 rule states that most of the time, eighty percent of the outputs come from twenty percent of the inputs. Those twenty percent must be finding its way in Category A.

Step 3. Find the activities listed in category A that can be smartly shifted to category B and find the activities listed in category C that can be shifted to category B or category D.

Step 4. After recategorizing the tasks, do the following:

Category A: Do more

Category B: Delegate immediately

Category C: Minimise or Delegate

Category D: Eliminate or Delegate

Do not spend more than one-fourth of your time on tasks not listed in Category A. Put your maximum effort into your core tasks. If, after a while, you see yourself spending more time on non-core tasks, rethink your categorization. Redo the above steps and learn leadership skills and effective delegation.

In exceptional situations, you may need to delegate your core task. It becomes essential when you consider more than justifiable tasks as core tasks. The idea is simple: Making the best use of time by doing what you should do, not what you can do, and by focusing your energy on what you do best. What you should do can never be bargained. However, what you can do can be delegated to others with supervision. This trade-off will leave you with more time for tasks that need your attention. It will improve your time management, efficiency, orderliness, and productivity.

There should be a specific focus on reducing managerial activities, especially meetings. A lot of times, we can't understand why we are in a particular session. It isn't that we are not interested in the job. But many times we don't find it useful. As per the largest conference service provider

Intercall, during conference calls, at one point in time, 65% of the employees are doing other works, 55% are eating or cooking food, and 43% of them are using social media.[23.2]

Another survey on 182 senior managers reported in Harvard Business Review brought out that 71% managers think meetings are unproductive and inefficient, 65% think meetings keep them from completing their own work, and 64% said meetings come at the expense of deep thinking.[23.3] Meetings take up more than a justifiable amount of employee's time. Though it keeps employees engaged and gives constant discussion and checks on progress, it generally does not produce the expected results. Indeed, one study found that CEOs, on average, have 37 meetings a week that makeup 72% of their total work time. Most CEOs also believe one-hour meetings can be reduced to 15-30 minutes meetings.[23.4]

The apparent trick to conduct shorter meetings is to distribute the data beforehand. Before the meeting, talk yourself through the situations that might erupt and prepare yourself and your team by giving them pre-meeting information to help them come up with constructive solutions. Have a clear agenda and be clear of the questions you want to get answered by the end of the discussion. Do not tolerate anyone who hasn't come prepared. Keep it specific and serious.

Successful companies aren't successful because their founders thought they would do everything themselves. They became successful because they developed the modus operandi to run their business efficiently, even in their absence. They figured out what they can do better, got their team, outsourced their non-core activities, and kept aside the essentials for themselves. Of course, they started small, and everyone has to, but staying small is no one's ultimate goal. Don't fill up your days with ancillary activities. Distinguish the core and non-core tasks to know areas you need to focus on. Occupying yourself with ventures that generate half the income you would otherwise earn is nothing but stupidity. Making the best use of your time and energy is your responsibility.

Delegation isn't just about assigning the work. It's also about who you assign it to. Do they love it? Are they dedicated? And have you assigned it properly? It works best when it gets combined with good leadership skills. APJ Abdul Kalam, the former president of India, says, "Leader has to adopt a delicate balance between the hands-on and hands-off approach. The hands-on approach takes an active interest on a very regular basis in the members' work. The hands-off approach trusts team members and recognizes their need for autonomy to carry out their roles as they see fit. It hinges on their self-motivation. When the Leader goes too far with the hands-on approach, he is seen as an anxious and inferring type. If he goes too far hands-off, he is seen as abdicating his responsibility or not being interested".[23.5] The balance between these approaches allows your teammates to be more hard-working, creative, and responsible. It helps you make them future-ready. By delegating your work and making them accountable, you make them feel they contribute more than ever and are trusted even with the most critical tasks.

We all find it very hard to allocate time. Even a school-going kid these days finds it hard to find the time, let alone the family's breadwinner. Amidst all the engagements and commitments in one's life, even a minute of extra work seems crushing. This is when prioritizing and delegating becomes all the more crucial. It's the only way to take control of your life. Hit the bullseye. Say no to the tasks that don't deserve your precious attention and delegate the task that can be done by others.

Action Challenge: *Set a specific priority for the next seven days. If you are bound to have two priorities, divide your day into two parts and use each segment for working on one priority. If it suits you, make this mechanism a part of your life.*

To understand the process of delegation further, refer to Part 6 - "An easy mechanism to delegation" of the workbook.

CHAPTER TWENTY-FOUR

THE GIFTS OF ISOLATION

"The only people who believe thinking is easy are those who don't habitually engage in it."

-John C. Maxwell

Look at a tumbler of water. What do you feel when you find particles suspended in it, and the water looks clear? To the naked eye, the crystal clarity of the water makes it seem drinkable. Likewise, in life, the clarity of thoughts make our goals achievable. Once we attain clarity, translating the thought into a desire, and the desire into action becomes a natural phenomenon. Driving your vehicle, which is your body, to the place of your desire, becomes much easier when you fuel your vehicle with clarity. When it is clouded inside, the world around you looks hazy. But once you are clear about what you want, you get clear about what you need to do.

Bill Gates is famously known to have 'think weeks' in which he isolates himself to a small cabin in the woods (except the helper to serve food) for two weeks, once a year. He takes all the essential documents and a stack of books to go through during his 'think weeks'. This isolation led to the pioneering advent of Tablet-PC's, among others.

Something of that sort was also practiced by Japan's richest man. When Masayoshi Son, the founder of Japanese conglomerate Softbank, was in college, he decided to allow himself five minutes a day for activities other than studies. He asked his friends, "Isn't there a good job through which I can earn $10000 p.m. in five minutes a day?". They said, "You are crazy, it's impossible. You wanna sell drugs?". He said, "No no I don't want to do that". He then started to contemplate what would be the most efficient use of his time. He realized that if he could invent something and file a patent, he could make good money. In the following days, he spent five minutes every morning at 5 o'clock prodding his mind for ideas. And one fantastic day, he became the inventor of the first electronic dictionary, which he sold for a whopping $1.7 million. He did not stop with that. His next project fetched him another $1.5 million. He later started SoftBank with $3.2 million, which he earned in 18 months by only setting aside five minutes of think time every day.[24.1] Finding five minutes for thinking is no big deal. Alternatively, you may also set aside thirty minutes of think time once a week.

What do you think you can do in 13 hours of isolation? 13 hours to most of us might sound pretty less in terms of being able to turn it into a game-changer. It's like having a day of isolation with more than justifiable time to sleep and finish the chores. Most of us won't spend more than five hours of productive sessions in the same amount of time. However, Dr. David Rock, CEO of The Neuroleadership Institute, has a different story to tell. Dr. Rock, being well aware of the importance of isolation, makes most use of it during his flights. He wrote four books during his several flights between to and from Australia, having the chance for complete focus. He knows our brain performs better without distraction and embraces all opportunities to make the most of his isolation.[24.2]

Unfortunately, all of us do not have the luxury to isolate ourselves to a secluded scenic spot with a caretaker to serve us meals or to book a flight to eliminate distraction. But we surely can figure out ways to isolate ourselves from the noise of our surroundings. This beneficial isolation is more about what you escape from and what you escape to than where you escape to. Isolation need not necessarily be a stay away from your family. It could also be a disconnection from social media for a while. It could be for a few hours a day or could last for days, weeks, months, or years. Isolation need not be time-bound. It could also be permanent, depending upon the cause. Isolating yourself from negative people is one such example of permanent isolation.

In reality, social networking applications like Instagram, Facebook, or Twitter may not be useful to everyone. Apart from people like celebrities who endorse their brands or companies that market their products or people who use these platforms to aid their business, most of us like and share posts that have no bearing on our lives. Yet, even those who have this realization find it challenging to keep these distractions from hogging their time. But, when you resolve to isolate yourself from these addictive time bandits, you give the best gift to your mind - a deep sense of relaxation from the compulsive urge to tap fingers on the digital screen for no reason. Try it out just for two days to experience this real joy. There are always alternatives available to communicate important stuff.

Overcome your FOMO (Fear of Missing Out, as they call it!). There's nothing great you're going to miss in that week's time. Your well-wishers will never hate you for not joining them for dinner. They understand you and are always wishing for your success and happiness. Initially, some might get irritated by your behavior, but that's not going to last long. After all, you aren't leaving them because you hate them. You are doing this to have a better time with them. And those who don't support you are anyway not important.

The legend of basketball, Michael Jordan, says, "To be successful, you have to be selfish, or else you never achieve. And once you get to your highest level, then you have to be unselfish. Stay reachable. Stay in touch. Don't isolate". Isolating yourself for a while every now and again, during your pursuit for success, is one way of being selfish to achieve, which even legends like Jordan concur with. Plan to have a few hours/days as DND now and then. Make it clear to everyone that you will not be available during that time. Remember, your big project requires a big commitment. Don't trade it for your responsiveness.

In the footsteps of Bill and Masayoshi, set aside "think time" once or twice a week and isolate yourself to make the most of it. Think about any topic of your choice ranging from personal problems to professional issues. You can utilize this time not only to solve your problems but also to come up with fresh ideas. Once you start practicing, you will amaze yourself with the results. To best utilize this time, keep yourself at ease. Do not push yourself too much into thinking about one aspect. Let the ideas flow through your mind naturally and grab them on their passing. Jot them down immediately in your notepad. You may use the Pomodoro app if your work requires systematic thinking and plan several minutes of think time multiple times a day. But, remember not to get swayed away by emotions. Many people make the mistake of getting overpowered by their thoughts. Don't let your think time become your sulk time. Isolate such hard feelings, focus your mind on the problem you want to solve, create solutions, and work on them.

Action Challenge: Schedule the tasks given below:

1. For the next one week, work for at least ninety minutes a day in complete isolation.

Time :

2. Set aside thirty minutes to think on one significant problem you are currently facing.

Time :

CHAPTER TWENTY-FIVE

TIME THIEVES

"I recommend you to take care of the minutes, for the hours will take care of themselves."

-Philip Dormer Stanhope

Where do you waste most of your time? I know what you are thinking-social media, emails, television, phone calls, partying, chit-chatting, etc. But is that true? Probably not. You may disagree, but the truth is we waste the maximum of our time in "DOING NOTHING."

Many of the people are not doing anything a lot of the time. People either procrastinate or mull over things that are not worth their time. Don't fall prey to this category. Time is not your puppet to dance at your whim. It just flies without your notice.

When I heard about this "doing nothing" thing around eight years ago, I got an eyeful of my time killers. Though I did waste a lot of time watching television and scrolling Facebook, I noticed that I spent even more time doing nothing. I had decided that I would rather eat my ice cream before it melts. Initially, when I started being judicious with my time, I was astounded at how much time I had in my hand. Sadly, even today, I feel there is still a minuscule amount of my time, which gets wasted doing nothing.

A study conducted by psychologists Matthew Killingsworth and Daniel Gilbert found that humans spend forty-seven percent of their waking hours "mind wandering."[25.1] Say if you are awake for sixteen hours and your mind wanders for seven hours, you are only left with eight hours to do constructive work. Let's say you are unlike most of the population, and your mind wanders only for half of the time research has found, and you are awake sixteen hours a day. That still says you are wasting five days a month mindlessly wandering without having anything pertinent to think about. Don't believe it? Try this out. Keep a sheet of paper handy while working on your most important task. Put a tick mark every time a random thought crosses your mind. You need not do this for hours to understand its impacts. Try it for a few minutes and see for yourself how many times you get distracted due to infertile thoughts. You may also try it now while reading this chapter.

Let's understand that there's a difference between constructive thinking and mindlessly wandering. Constructive thinking can bridge gaps in various aspects of life while mindlessly wandering by exaggerating scenarios in your head, worrying, daydreaming, negative thinking, and chit-chatting with self, decimate you. It not only makes you unproductive, but it also sabotages your composure. Disorders such as depression and anxiety often occur in association with stressful events. Most of the stress that we put on ourselves is just an outcome of our delusions. If we learn to live in the moment, we would never go into depression. Being present in the moment is called consciousness that can be learned and practiced through meditation. Deepak Chopra, an advocate of alternative-medicine, says, "Meditation is not a way of making your mind quiet. It's a way of entering into the quiet that's already there – buried under the 50,000 thoughts the average person thinks every day".

Notice whenever your mind starts to wander. Stop it there itself. It would be challenging initially, but you can develop the ability to be present at the moment with practice. The best way to stop mind-wandering is by tackling it the second it starts. Whenever you realize that you have gone astray, get into action. Even if you have to do it a hundred times, do it and bring it back to work. Don't entertain impertinent thoughts. Remind yourself of the futility in such a drift. Act on things laid in front of you. Shift your attention and focus on the 'now.' Don't worry about what's not real. Even if the situation stands for real, it may not be present right now. And if it's present right now, better deal with it. Leadership coach Robin Sharma says, "Most people I have spoken to have no idea that they have the power to control every single thought they think every second of every minute of every day. They believe that thoughts just happen and have never realized that if you don't take the time to start controlling your thoughts, they will control you".

Apart from mind wandering, there are a few other factors that sweep your time off without your permission. Needless worrying, caving into unnecessary distractions, meetings without agenda, ineffective delegation, etc., are some of the time thieves that consume a gluttonous amount of time and yet produce exiguous results.

According to research conducted by Bain and Company, an organization spends fifteen percent of its time in meetings. This percentage has been increasing every year since 2008. That's not all. Social media giants like Facebook and WhatsApp have encroached on all aspects of our lives, including our work life. The usage of social media during work hours has quadrupled. Employees claim their work hours have increased due to the use of social media during office time. Emails have their own story and so do lunch breaks. With a lot on our platter to distract us from the main course, it's a ride up rocky terrain to stay focused.

We look at the time all the time, but we are not attentive enough to track the duration expended on a particular activity. We do not invariably account for the time spent doing needless tasks such as setting up the desk, waiting for a call or an email, clearing out the clutter, or just getting in the mood. To be clear, I have nothing against clean desks or good moods. I want us to be cognizant of these potential 'time leaks' that creep in subtly, without our notice. We heedlessly ignore these leaks being the minutiae of everyday life. However, their cumulative effect over twenty-four hours may surprise you as you find out that we have been wasting around 2.34 hours a day just catching up with emails[25.2], 35 minutes deciding what to eat[25.3] and 16 minutes deciding what to wear.[25.4]

There is a fair amount of time in our routine that can be saved if we learn to make things simpler. Having fewer clothes, keeping things organized and handy, eating foods that are easy to prepare, not wasting time while ordering, setting up office bags in a way that we need not worry about it every day, and practicing minimalism can save a reasonable amount of time for anyone.

However, to get hold of your time, try tracking the entire day for a week to understand how you are using your twenty-four hours. Use your office camera or install a personal camera to observe yourself for a week. If that's not possible, write your activities in a diary. Note the activities to be added/replaced/eliminated and take the appropriate action. In any business, the focus is to optimize the efforts to get optimal profits. Blue-chip companies like Amazon have mastered the art of chipping in less and whipping out more. They have done it to such an extent that their workers claim to be treated like robots. In fact, they are monitored via robots. Imagine how that would feel- a robot as your supervisor. Ignoring the moral science of whether Amazon is doing the right thing, its impeccable productivity has catapulted it into the limelight.

Most of the successful people have developed a policy of not getting into contentious conversations. Rarely do they comment on controversial subjects like politics. Even when they do, they resort to diplomacy. They are inclined to avoid silly scuffles with anyone. They choose to think before they act rather than act and then repent. They don't find a sense of achievement in winning futile arguments. They stay poised and indifferent to the extraneous happenings around the world. They develop these saint-like characteristics to build the dream they have seen. They choose to focus on their vision and keep aside everything that might derail their energy. Likewise, if you have dared to dream and are determined to live up to it, you need to give up on petty issues and save your time for quintessential endeavors.

Time thieves don't just come up in the form of extra activity or a noticeable disturbance. A small distraction can also disrupt our concentration. Often, while working, we find ourselves getting distracted by petty things. Our brain keeps reminding us of the tasks we need to accomplish. We might have to wish someone on their birthday or buy groceries while returning home. Our mind never stops evoking these thoughts irrespective of what we are doing. The more service-based job you have, the higher the brain pounds for the variety of unfinished tasks, like replying to an email, connecting the customer to an agent, sending a report, and like that.

To address these distractions for the moment, consider writing out what's disturbing on a piece of paper. This technique tricks the brain into thinking that the thought train is archived and will be dealt with accordingly. It frees the mind from the continuous pounding and allows us to focus on the task at hand. If it's something you can finish in minutes, do it, otherwise write them down and settle them later.

Another silent thief is multitasking. Can you solve a math problem while you are involved in a fistfight? If you are a math geek, then you might end up losing a tooth. But what if you are working on a research project while chatting with your friend. This time, though your teeth are intact, there's an impediment to your performance to which most turn a blind eye.

When we think we are doing two tasks simultaneously, our brain skips back and forth between the designated tasks. De facto, our brain processes just one task at a time. This implies human multitasking, in a way, is a myth. If a person is proficient in multitasking, it means he can rapidly shift his attention between the designated tasks. In most cases, it only results in wastage of time and commission of errors due to insufficient attention. As said by Steve Uzzell, "Multitasking is nearly the opportunity to screw up more than one thing at a time."

Though a computer with a decent amount of RAM can steer its way by multitasking, a human brain that can outsmart a computer in specific ways is never good at it. The human brain performs its best when it focuses on one task at a time. Earl Miller, a cognitive neuroscientist and a professor at MIT, says, "When people think they're multitasking, they're actually just switching from one task to another very rapidly. And every time they do, there's a cognitive cost in doing so."

This impact of cognitive cost can be seen in the research conducted by Sophie Leroy, demonstrating the effect of task switching. The study found that when people leave their previous tasks halfway, their performance also suffers in their next task. That's because the human brain keeps thinking about unfinished tasks leading to attention residue, a term coined by Leroy. She says people need to stop thinking about a task to fully transition their attention and perform well on the other. Her study also proves that when people complete the previous task, they perform better on the next task because of increased confidence.[25.5]

These days listening to audiobooks while driving has much been talked about due to long mundane commute time. But is it working even when you are the one behind the wheel? It can because listening to podcasts is a passive activity that gives room for your brain to allocate its cognitive abilities to drive. Listening persistently to similar ideas helps us implant it in our subconscious. Stimulating the subconscious mind catalyzes a shift in our mindset. And that way, it works. Even marketing studies say that verbal advertisements have more impact on the consumer's subconscious mind than visuals advertisements, which is why radio is still being used as a medium of advertising to tap the consumer's subconscious inference. However, this is not the case if you listen to a math theorem while driving, as both these tasks are active and require the brain's cognitive abilities to process. As a consequence, you can hardly follow any of them.

The process of identifying your' time thieves' and 'time leaks' can bring forth a range of activities that can be tackled smartly. However, the progress could be proliferated only when you act upon them. I am sure you could come up with little things to optimize your time, which could fetch you a great deal in terms of results. You need not do this daily. Try this exercise for a week, say, once every six months, and take immediate action to optimize your time. When you rescue time, the rescued time will come to your rescue!

Action Challenge: *Become aware of the total time (T) you have. Track the time you spend effectively (E) throughout the day. The difference between T and E is the time you end up doing nothing (N). Become aware of this time burglar. The Rule of Ten: T - E = N Total time (T) - Effective Time (E) = Doing Nothing Time (N).*

CHAPTER TWENTY-SIX

DITCH THE WANDERING, GO STRAIGHT!

We deserve happiness, and that is indubitable. But what makes us happy? To many of us, it's to binge-watch our favorite shows on Netflix. Some rave that they are party animals. A few seek happiness in material possessions. Some love to sleep. We are indeed immensely 'pleasured' doing such things, but how often do we experience 'happiness'? A relaxed lifestyle, tension-free days, goal-less period keeps us at 'peace.' But if one thinks that he is embracing 'happiness' in that, then he is acutely mistaken as such pleasures are just an illusion that one creates in mind to save oneself from the hassles of hard work. Despite realizing this, many people still seek 'pleasure' instead of 'happiness,' let alone 'eternal' happiness.

If there's pleasure in passing the time, then there's happiness in utilizing time. If you love sleeping, observe the difference in the sense of satisfaction that you get when you sleep after a day's good work and after a day's goofing around. Even our leisure gives us the right pleasure only when it is after a period of good work.

Though many things make us happy, nothing can ever surpass the level of happiness we can get from achieving our goals. Despite requiring us to work our ass off, it makes us happiest the most. So if you are seeking pleasure, keep wandering. But if you are seeking happiness, you should set your goals right now!

I often hear from certain people that they are happy in their lives, and hence there's no reason for them to aim high. When I come across them, I ask them this question: are you happy WITH your life? They would give me a perplexed look and say, "didn't we just say that?" There's a difference between being happy IN life and being happy WITH life. Being happy IN life is your reaction to the situations in your life. Being happy WITH life is the satisfaction you derive when you can turn your life the way you desire. You can be happy IN life if you are complacent. But mostly you cannot be happy WITH life unless you reach your goals. Some of you must have attained both kinds of happiness. But some prefer short term happiness by resorting to complacency to avoid straining themselves for reaching their future goals. Don't get me wrong. I am not against staying happy, no matter how the situations are in your life. I just don't want you to renounce your goals for the sake of temporary comfort.

Many people deceive themselves into thinking that they don't have a goal at all. That can't be true. Everybody has a goal, big or small, written or not, admitted or not. You could be off track, you could be ineffective, or you could be unproductive. But you can never be without a goal. A man without a goal is a man without a desire. But a man without a desire is a myth, for there's a desire even in being ascetic. People think they don't have a goal when their actions are a product of their goals, which is an outcome of a desire. Be it a goal of buying a new house or going on a vacation or social service, or maintaining a high standard of living, it's always present even though it's not recognized or written. Otherwise, why would someone work forty-eight hours a week, why would someone take the extra effort to get promoted, or why would someone go the extra mile to get a new client? All this effort proves that there is a goal behind your actions. The place where we go wrong is not being able to realize and embrace its presence. The more specific and more explicit the goals are, the more productive and effective your actions will be.

Goals could be big or small. It could be as small as buying A car. It could be as big as buying THE car. Big or small is more of your perspective than its physicality. Big or small, it has to be written. Often people strain away from writing goals and despise working on that format. A goal, which is just a thought in your mind, is never effective unless given a physical manifestation. So write it, look at it every day, meditate on it and work on it till you attain it. It's okay if you don't want to have a big goal but ensure that achieving your goals fulfill your desire, one step at a time, with persistence to follow-through.

Most of us are working on our short term goals. It's sporadic to find people who are clear about what they want in the long run. I request you to hustle yourself into deep contemplation. Use your core values. Think of the factors that affect you and give you real happiness. Spend some extra time thinking about what you want out of your life and find your medium and long term goals. Align your short term goals with your long term goals, and don't worry if you find your dream changing in the next few days. It's a part of the process. Embrace it by molding your actions.

Before you write your goals, let us understand and redefine what a goal means. Let's say you have an upcoming deadline in five days, and you have to finish it to avoid being fired. If that's the condition, you do it anyway. Let's take another example, you are going on a trekking trip, and you have to board a flight in the evening, which means you need to prepare yourself before you leave. Again, as the plan is predefined, you do it without a doubt. You do not question whether you should pack your bag or a cab for the airport. Since you are clear about what you should do, you do it .

Whenever you set a goal, set it with the level of seriousness you show when asked to do it at gunpoint. Set it with the intention to genuinely achieve it. Don't decide on something because you are supposed to do it. Decide on it because you mean to do it.

The problem with goals is that when we don't accomplish them, there are no measurable real-time losses, and that debases our solemnity towards it. We tend to compromise on them. We think, "It's fine, I will do it later," and procrastination never gets us anywhere. We do not lack time and capability to achieve our goals, we lack seriousness while setting them. We lack seriousness while working on them.

Firstly, you need to take each goal very rigorously. You need to understand that if you keep missing your goals, it will become a habit. And just so you don't make it your habit, you need to take the tiniest of the goals with utter seriousness. If the circumstances have changed, then that's a different story, but usually, circumstances don't change so often. Ask yourself, is it the circumstance, or are you justifying your wavering attitude towards life? Most often, things stay the same, and so should be your action and determination towards your goals.

Secondly, you need to make sure that you don't overextend your goals. Pushing your limits, on the contrary, is one thing that helps you realize your new capabilities in the shortest period. But extending it to the extent, you feel that you have already lost the race would be counterproductive. With a little appetite to beat your limits, you plan for the impossible in its most real sense. You might finish it if you try to, but the efficacy could be lost. If numbers are the name of the game, that could work. However, it's not most of the time.

The third advice, probably one of the finest you can get on goal setting, is to have less of them. If you want to be better, go for three goals; if you are smart, go for two; and if you have the courage, go for one! But never go for more than three at a time. Having too many goals is equivalent to having no goals. If you don't believe how much it can change things for you, just for one day, try focusing only on a single goal. Spend all your waking hours on that goal with 100% focus, and you will be amazed by your result. In this race of achieving everything, we have lost focus. Remember, the race is not to achieve EVERYTHING. It is to accomplish THE THING. One of the things that all the successful people have in common is that they don't try to do everything right. They only focus on doing one thing right. Trying different things, failing, and realizing your mistakes isn't a problem. It is a part of the process to get what you want. However, once you have figured out the path you want to follow, you need not walk different roads.

To understand this further, refer to Part 7 of Workbook- Goal Finder.

Lastly, you need to sincerely adhere to your deadlines. Napoleon Hill said, "Goals are dreams with deadlines." With the ever-increasing use of a to-do list, a deadline is what puts things into perspective. Without a time frame, there wouldn't be any sense of priority. The corporate culture is dead set to work against deadlines. There's always a race to finish the projects quicker than their peers. There's no denying that there's a grievous amount of deadlines present in this sector. This is one of the reasons why the corporate sector fetches more results in comparison to others. None of the projects gets assigned without a deadline. As we know that a project without a deadline is a project with no end in sight. No profit-oriented company would be willing to pay salaries for getting less work done.

Set a realistic deadline to realize your goals. Nothing too lax or too stern. Allow yourself to be flexible enough to have breathing space in between. At times, big goals could be intimidating, a vivid vision could be daunting, and expectations could be overwhelming. But remember one thing, you need not make great strides every time. Modest consistent strides will also get you to your destination.

To create your strides, start by planning your days. None of the successful businesses you see has thrived without a plan. Of course, most of the time, all of the plans fail. Yet, one cannot afford to skip this process. The high failure rate is because of improper planning and should not be attributed to the process of planning itself.

Plans are vital to keeping you on track. Instead of planning for a month or a week, plan for the next three days every three days. Because when we try to plan for a whole week/month, most of us forget what the plan was by the middle of it—no wonder why things do not go as planned. Even when you stick it on your refrigerator and keep an eye on it, it doesn't make much difference. So it's better to plan for something workable, crisp, easy to remember, and much easier to abide by.

It's typical for executives and managers to plan their entire week as most of their schedule is clear. They know whom to meet, where to go, and how long a meeting might last. They have a personal secretary to schedule their time and remind them of their upcoming task. However, in this not so perfect world, the next ten hours itself is tough to predict for an ordinary person. You don't have that lovely secretary to rely on. You are your secretary.

Daily plans are equally troublesome as a lot of us are bad at estimating the amount of work we can do in a day. Thus, it becomes irritating after a while to have a daily planner. A planner should be short, clear and flexible.

Plan for the next three days every three days. Write down your top two goals. You may choose more than two, but do not exceed three. It becomes overwhelming for our brain when it has to process an awful lot of information. Instead, give it a few tasks and let it strive for excellence. Make sure your goals are a tiny subset of your short, medium, and long term goals. Be specific about the things you want to get accomplished. Write down three to four tasks you need to finish for each goal and consider the end of three days as your deadline for the tasks written. Do not forget to check how much you accomplished and start making better plans by learning from your past mistakes.

To understand this further, refer to Part 8 - My Next 3 of the Workbook.

Take the lead in your life by distinguishing between pleasure and happiness. Contemplate well to have a clear long term goal. See for yourself whether your daily activities and short term goals are well aligned with your long term goals. Have fewer goals. Plan your days. Stick to your deadlines and sweat over till you accomplish them. Let failure not stop you. Show that you're beyond it. One last thing, do not be afraid to dream big.

Action Challenge: *Contemplate on your long term goals for thirty minutes. Do not limit yourself because of your current circumstances. Aim high.*

FIGHT THE PHONE ADDICTION

Have you ever imagined what you could have learned in the past five years had you given yourself just one area to work on every month? We are not talking about developing expertise over an area. We are talking about learning everyday skills like speaking, grooming, personal branding, swimming, etc. There are so many things we can do if we give ourselves monthly targets. If you had started doing this five years ago, you could have worked on 60 different skills. If that sounds too much, 20 skills in five years was definitely a workable idea. You could have been 100% better in at least ten areas.

Think of the things you learned at work in the past five years without having the deliberate goal to learn it. You learned it because you spent time on it. Giving an hour to yourself out of work for the topics that interest you is the easiest thing you can do to make the most of your days. But do you remember what you did with the time you could have devoted to these activities? For most of you, I am sure one activity that killed your time was definitely social media. Others could be binge-watching, hangouts, online shopping, gaming, etc.

Isn't it interesting that some of us feel obliged to watch series as if something in our life would go missing if we don't watch it? Aren't we ready to sacrifice more than what it genuinely deserves? Okay, some series might be special to us. But what about others? Just because we have heard good things about it, does it mean it deserves our precious time? Think about the opportunity costs these menial activities carry with them. Think about what you could have done had you invested your time wisely.

These days binge-watching, social media, youtube, and shopping apps have become the biggest threat to our productivity. The chemical that makes one a drug addict is also causing these addictions. It's called dopamine, an organic chemical responsible for transmitting signals between our nerve cells. It is famously known as the "happy hormone," which gets released even at a slight hint of pleasure. It's the same chemical that gets to work when the roulette in a casino starts to spin and keeps you playing even when you are losing money. Social media platforms, casinos, and junk food vendors are smartly using this science behind our brains to keep us coming back.

Today, social media captures over one-third of online time.[27.1] But why is it so difficult to resist using social media in the first place? That's because we all love attention. Our dopamine gets released whenever we see acceptance from someone. We love to be liked by people. Likes in our picture, comments on our status, birthday wishes from strangers, and even a flash of notification give us a constant urge to check it. Even if someone invites us to a boring event, we feel good about being invited, but the critical question to ask is: Is it making us any better? Is it taking us anywhere?

Social media is such a miraculous thing that if you don't learn to use it, you will get used by it. Businesses worldwide know how to sell fashion trends via Instagram, Cambridge Analytica knows how to buy votes via Facebook, preachers know how to create contagion via WhatsApp and Youtube knows how to make you stick to their platform for a longer time. If you aren't the one producing and selling your business idea, then surely you are the one consuming it. It's incredible to be a consumer when you genuinely want to be, but what if that's not the case? What if a salesperson intrudes into your house and tries to sell his product? What would you do? If things go out of control, you might even call the cops! Well, the same is happening in social media these days. Facebook is manipulating the election outcome. Everyone's status proclaims a pretentious life of their dreams when, in fact, they are no exception. After all, who gets to look through the veil? And here you wonder why your life sucks even despite having your fair share of good times. This reminds me of a funny incident. Once I traveled to Bangalore for an event in the Taj Hotel. Lying in my room, I was checking my WhatsApp status where I saw a picture of my cousin traveling to a new city having a great time. I suddenly felt a twinge of disappointment about my life as it seemed boring at that moment compared to my cousin. A second later, I realized where I was lying down; in a fabulous hotel in a happening city. Nothing was boring in that visit, nor was I sad about anything. I was having a great time too, yet someone else's status made me feel that I was living less.

These days social media has the power to toss your emotions upside down. It is nothing but making you want more and more and be dissatisfied with what you have. The constant peek into your role models' lifestyle and their fashion trends, the fantastic stories your friends are sharing, the urge to be more attractive is taking a toll on your self-esteem. Research suggests that with the rise of usage of social media, depression has risen too. One major reason is that social media connectivity is not able to leave us satisfied with the connections we have, even though we have it often. The deep compassionate feeling the physical contact creates is missing. Though it has helped us be in touch with our loved ones, it has also taken us far from the people present with us. The lack of oneness is making us feel dejected and isolated.

The way we are brought up has made us excessively dependent on society's validation, the love of our close ones, and the need for a constant reminder of being wanted and accepted. Growing above this validation would be great, but it might feel like an impossible solution to many. To address this basic need of being social creatures, we need to build genuine connections, stronger bonds, and be honest and authentic in our relations. As unless we have a fulfilling personal life, something will always eat us up inside.

Research conducted by the University of Pennsylvania has found that "limiting social media usage does have a direct and positive impact on subjective wellbeing over time, especially with respect to loneliness and depression."[27.2] The world of social media looks fancy but do not get caught up by this marketing. The CEOs of these applications are doing their job perfectly, and I think it's time we should too.

The inordinate reliance on smartphones has reached to such an extent that it has led to the coining of a new term called "Nomophobia" by the UK Post Office in 2010 to explain the fear of living without a phone. UK Post commissioned a research organization named YouGov to study the anxiety caused by mobile phones. They found that fifty three percent of mobile phone users in Britain get anxious when they lose their phone or when it stops working due to battery shortage or no network area.

Today, there are more smartphone users than people with access to toilets. The developers deliberately build the apps in such a way that it becomes impossible to get over them. They know how to get us hooked. They form a habit loop by ensuring the presence of three elements: a cue, a routine, and a reward. They design a cue that triggers a routine and gives us rewards to make us come back. A survey states that an average person between the ages of eighteen and twenty-four checks their smartphones about eighty-six times a day, even when there's no notification to lure them.[27.3]

One of the basic premises of productivity is reducing the clutter around. Until we develop the practice to deliberately shut-off ourselves from this constant noise, at least during our peak productive hours, we wouldn't be able to make the best use of our energy. We must turn off the notifications or reminders to resist the strong pull. The sheer amount of information that gets bombarded on us quickly becomes overbearing. If we allow it, it can consume our entire day, and there'd still be more information to process.

With the way smartphones and digitization have transformed the world, it would be unjustifiable to degrade its significance. But everything comes with a cost that can not be ignored. However, it can be optimized. If you are one of those who have the compulsive urge to check your phone repeatedly, here are specific measures you can take to fight your phone addiction:
- Switch off all the app notifications.
- Hide the phone in your office drawer while working.
- Mute everyone on WhatsApp except a few important people.
- Uninstall social media apps on your cell phone.
- Set up time restrictions on addictive applications.

If none of the above points seems feasible, the best way to desist phone distraction is by placing your phone a little distant, although accessible (without silencing your phone, if required). The logic is simple- you can't control yourself from eating chocolates kept in front of you. Likewise, it becomes irresistible to check notifications when your phone is in front. When you don't see it, there's a chance that you won't think of it. You will forget it's existence at least for some time.

Walter Mischel, a psychologist at Stanford, conducted the famous marshmallow experiment. He made the five-year-old sit in an empty room with a marshmallow. The kids were told if they do not eat the marshmallow for fifteen minutes, they will get another one as a treat. Some kids ate it the very second, some tried to control themselves for a while and ate it after a few minutes, and some fought their instant gratification monkey to get the next one. The kids that could fight their instant gratification fought it by not looking into the marshmallow. They diverted their minds either by singing a song or covering their eyes, or pretending to play in the room. If something of your interest is kept in front of you, it's hard to fight your urge. However, when you hide it from your view, it becomes much easier to fight it off. Initially, your brain will remind you of its presence, but with some practice, you will be successful in distracting yourself.

Fighting your phone addiction is crucial because you can't grow beyond your compulsivity until you break this petty threshold. Today, most of the population is stuck with the routine matters of life. Be it socializing, being available, replying to emails, or looks. People are having a hard time overcoming these matters, which barely have any value. They aren't able to think beyond these less impactful activities of day to day life. However, once you grow above these little things, you will enter a different zone of life. Once you are out of your compulsivity, you will start to notice what matters. You will see things differently, and your inner drive will begin to surface. You will become aware of what you genuinely want and see a new self with real goals and missions. Right now, shopping and social media apps are having more control over your behavior than your minds. Fight them off and see how the other side of the world welcomes you.

Action Challenge: Keep your phone six feet away from your eyesight while working. If that's too much, hide it in your drawer.

CHAPTER TWENTY-EIGHT

KNOW THE "NO"

How often do you find yourself in a situation where you are not acting from your will? How many times in a year do you go to social events despite being uninterested? How many times do you say yes to someone when you want to say no? Warren Buffet says, "The difference between successful people and very successful people is that very successful people say no to almost everything."

Social interactions are an essential part of our existence. You'll always find someone who needs your help at a task or someone who has a fascinating story to tell. But sadly, the clock doesn't stop ticking. It waits for none. Learn to say no to unimportant matters, and people will stop disturbing you when you are busy. After all, if you don't value your own time, how can you expect everyone else to respect yours? You don't need to oblige every invitation. You don't have to listen to every story of your neighbor's or reply to all the phone calls. It is okay to respond with a no if it hinders your work firmly.

Mind it, when you are saying yes to others, you are saying no to yourself and your priorities. Decide what is more important- a phone call or the work in hand. Learn to say no firmly but at the same time be appreciative of the opportunities you are getting. Acknowledge the invitation, be thankful to the person, and say no gracefully. People will get used to a genuine no and will understand your reason behind it. They will respect you more as they see you value your time. People are not fools. They are good observers. It might take some time, but eventually, your actions are bound to be understood. History tells us that the one who makes appropriate use of time is more respected than the one available all the time. Of course, there will be some who will not be so appreciative of your decisions. Irrespective of how good you are and how genuinely you care for them, there will always be some people who would be sad, complaining, and making you feel bad for your choices. You can't change the statistics. Sometimes, people feel bad not because you did something wrong, but they feel bad because they aren't doing things right, they aren't having control over their emotions, and have got into a vicious cycle of overthinking and imagining situations and their outcome. It would be inappropriate to shoulder the responsibilities of others' feelings and emotions in such a case.

Saying no doesn't mean that you get offensive. It relies on the way you say it. It's an art to say no. The best way to do it is by showing full respect, praising, and acknowledging their offer. Once you learn this art, it will become more comfortable. I know what you are thinking, "it's easier said than done."

I recently met a friend at his office to discuss something important. Though our discussion ended in around an hour, I kept talking to him. He then admitted that it's his snack time and asked me if I would like to join him for a fresh juice. I, being in love with juices, nodded in agreement. We went downstairs. There was a juice stall just beside his office. We had our juice and then, of course, I had to leave!

The moment he admitted that he neeeds a glass of juice, it was apparent that he wanted me to leave. But I was impressed. My initial reaction was wow! That was a subtle way to tell that it's time for me to get out. I complimented him for this act, but of course, he denied it. However, he spilled the beans later that he learned it from his boss.

It's that easy to send someone out of your office. At the same time, impress upon someone how vital your time is. If the other one happens to be someone like me, they'd be all the more impressed by you.

Just a few days after getting thrown away subtly, I happened to visit another friend's office in a co-working space, who is also my client. I happened to be there for a seminar, but since I had to collect some documents from him, I called him and met him in his office. He was very welcoming, offered me tea, and handed over all the documents politely. That took us less than 10 minutes. I kept all the records in my bag and, instead of leaving, stirred a conversation.

Wonder what you would do if you had to toss someone out of your cabin in such a situation? Mind you, this time you don't even have time for juice! If it's a good friend, you could probably admit that you need to work. A lot of us might not do that until and unless it's urgent. Instead, we tend to lie about our next appointment.

And what did he say? He asked me, "Have you taken all the documents?". I said yes and remained seated. After 30 seconds, he asked me again, "Do you need anything else?". I was too dumb to figure it out as generally whenever we met, we talked for at least an hour. I thought he would like to talk more. I remained seated until he said, "Okay, then let's meet sometime outside." This time gladly, I understood! Again, while leaving, I was impressed with his technique and his dedication to his work. In my head, I said to myself, "I should use that too."

Both the friends I referred to knew how to say no respectfully. I never made the mistake of thinking that they don't like me or my presence. They are my good friends. Indeed, the right way to put it is - they are my good, focused, and smart friends who value their time. They don't just appear to value their time, they genuinely do it, and they make it very clear to everyone with their gestures and actions that they are striving for more and seriously interested in their work, and who doesn't like such people? These people are everyone's inspiration. They are well achieved, well respected, and truly loved by all.

Sometimes we are too shy to speak our minds. Even if it doesn't leave a wrong impression or even an impression, we try to avoid it, contemplating what others might think. Do you think people have time to think? When you don't have time to think about this question for 10 seconds, why do you think people would care if you don't join them for dinner? They are too busy with their commitments. There's a high probability a person would get more offended if you fail to say a clear no and make the situation awkward by making excuses.

While writing this book, I asked some of my friends to help me with research work, editing, and blogs. All of them eagerly said yes, yet, barely twenty percent of them continued to work with me. I couldn't figure out who was genuinely interested as they themselves seemed to be unsure. However, as they started to work less enthusiastically, I realized they were having a problem saying no. Being aware of how hard it is to say no, I voluntarily offered them a chance and made them comfortable to say so. It was bizarre for me to see how these fantastic people struggled for such a small act. As these events happened, I realized most of us do not think much while accepting an offer. We say yes without serious considerations and find innovative ways of ignoring the consequences to save ourselves from the embarrassment of rejecting it later. If you notice, you will realize, we do not find it hard to say no because we are worried about what others might think of us. Instead, we are reluctant to say no either because we aren't clear of our priorities or because saying no is just too new for us.

Be clear about your priorities. Be clear about the type of career you want, the parties you want to go to and the kind of people you would like to work with. As when you are not, you get swayed away with the appearance of every new opportunity. Be clear of your priorities to be smartly able to wipe off the variety of choices you get presented daily.

Develop the habit to say no. Yes, I mean habit. You will find many people, including yourself, beating around the bush rather than being honest about your priorities. Do not say yes mindlessly to things you could have easily said no. Nobody really cares. Get above that thought.

Here is a simple mechanism to distinguish between the say yes activities and say no activities. This mechanism will save a lot of energy you spent wondering if you made the right decision. The mechanism asks you to only say yes to the activities that are a part of either of three categories and communicate a clear 'no' to everything else. The three categories are:

Category 1. Dreams: Shall involve all the activities that take you closer to your dreams. Example: studies, skill enhancement, business, job, gathering knowledge, reading articles, etc.

Category 2. Wellness: Anything that is essential to take care of your health. Example: Sleeping, napping, eating, cleansing, workout, meditation, yoga, sports, etc.

Category 3. Enjoyment: Any activity that brings you joy and happiness. Example: Parties, clubbing, social service, volunteering, vacations, hobbies, movies, shopping, etc.

If you notice, you will find that, usually, the activities that hamper your productivity don't fall in any of these categories. Those are the ones you should avoid saying yes. Here are some examples: parties that you don't enjoy, socializing which doesn't make you happy, excessive use of social media, unnecessary chit-chatting, gossiping, listening to others' stories, meetings, boring seminars, entertaining passerby's, etc. None of us embrace these activities, albeit we give ourselves up to these activities. We do it to please others, not ourselves. We do it out of compulsion, without much thought of why we are doing it. These activities have become a regular part of our life because we unconsciously resorted to squandering our time rather than utilizing it. The morose part of this disposition is that even the fun we perceive in doing such activities fades into regret later. However, developing the habit of appraising and categorizing any activity before we do it can keep us from being regretful later. This internal checklist can not only make us organized in our day to day life, but it can also save our irreplaceable time, which we have been killing in the name of blending in.

The act of balancing these categories is the decisive factor here. Certain times one might overdo the activities in one category to the extent that it disarrays the other parts of one's life. To be productive, you have to have an equilibrium. You got to work on your priorities, take care of your body well, and participate in activities that bring you joy than mere pleasure.

The examples of Category 1: Dreams, though, include almost all activities relevant to your career. Finding the activity that needs to be on your priority right now is vital. Attaining a Ph.D., enhancing your knowledge, working nine to five, etc. can surely elevate your career, but the critical question to ask is: Are they the fastest and smartest way to fulfill your dreams?

What would you choose to do if you had full liberty? Any activity that doesn't fulfill the answer should be eliminated. To fulfill your dreams, you need to prioritize and say no to all other choices.

Also, there is one area in this checklist where most of us have a problem, Category 3: Enjoyment. The problem is with the amount of consumption. You could always go to the limit but never beyond the limit. This limit is the frontier separating recreation from addiction. No research ever claimed that watching television makes people bright or playing video games guarantees good health. The study does suggest the opposite.

Fortunately, the addicts have no reason to back their addiction. You could justify to others that your addiction is merely an activity in check. But you can never explain it to yourself. You are your best judge. Impulsivity could lead to addiction, and compulsivity could strengthen it. Both impulsivity and compulsivity are results of poor self-control. Whether it's from an external or an internal source, the wrong thoughts you plant in your mind could play with your intelligence. To put it in other words, it all starts with not saying 'no' to things that don't deserve your time.

I have made it a point to abide by this internal categorical checklist. It gives me clear direction as to what is right for me at any point in time. It makes choosing my activities an affable affair. It declutters my schedule and creates time for my sincere bids. The above categorization also excludes activities like doing chores, which could be delegated but never eliminated. But you can minimize even such activities by racking your brains. This philosophy of saying 'no' along with mindfulness can guide you exceptionally well in filling up your calendar with activities that bridge the gap between you and your destination.

I personally follow the above mechanism very strictly. In simple words it says, if you are going to a party, enjoy every bit of it; if you are working, immerse into it and the rest of the time nourish every cell of your body. The rule is simple: say 'NO' to things that get you nowhere. This way you will never regret your choices and will live a life you want to live.

Action Challenge: Write down three activities to which you will be saying 'no' today onwards.

CHAPTER TWENTY-NINE

WORKBOOK

PART 1: Bird's eye view of your productivity

Given below is a series of questions in psychometric format. Rate them from 0 to 4 as applicable to you. Answer as objectively as possible. The rating system is as follows: 0- Strongly Disagree 1- Disagree 2- Neither Disagree nor Agree 3- Agree 4- Strongly Agree

After answering the questions, add your score and check the category you fit in. Each category has specific suggestions that can be implemented to enhance your productivity. Naturally, all other suggestions are still well-grounded. But as per your applicable category, certain actions are bound to produce better results than others. These questions will give you a bird's eye view of your current level of productivity.

1 Are you generally unsure of your decisions?

2 Do you criticize yourself too much?

3 Do you feel a lack of guidance?

4 Do you perform better when you are accountable to others?

5 Do you dislike Mondays?

6 Do you work extensively without short breaks in between?

7 Do you give inadequate time to physical fitness?

8 Do you lack clarity in your thoughts?

9 Do you hang out with people you dislike?

10 Are you accompanied by people who do not reflect your future?

11 Is self help absent from your daily agenda?

12 Does something eat you up inside very often?

13 Do you have poor/unhealthy lifestyle choices? (Excessive sleeping, unhealthy eating, too much alcohol consumption?)

14 Do you check social media within thirty minutes of waking up?

15 Do you fight/argue for petty stuff?

16 Do you lack consistency?

17 Do you procrastinate too often?

18 Do you get overwhelmed by the sheer number of daily tasks you have to do?

19 Does lack of specific tools and poor seating arrangement hamper your optimal performance?

20 Are your mornings filled with menial tasks?

21 Do you daydream too much?

22 Do you fail to set weekly/daily goals?

23 Do you spend more than an hour on social media everyday?

24 Do you face difficulty in concentrating?

25 Are you short of motivation/drive to succeed?

Total

RESULT (Set of practices to follow immediately):

Category 1 (0-10): Perfect. The good thing is there's always scope for improvement. All the best.

- Find a mentor.
- Take the first three hours of your morning very seriously.
- Nap once a day.
- Add a think time to your routine.
- Practice focus week.
- Have lesser goals and magnify your focus on your priorities.

Category 2 (11-30): Keep it up. Be consistent and keep learning.

- Take steps towards personal development- read, listen to audiobooks, attend seminars and courses.
- Spend more time with people who have already accomplished what you want.
- Have a clear vision.
- Eat five servings of fruits and vegetables everyday.
- Practice mindfulness.
- Avoid unnecessary meetings, parties, and chit chats.

Category 3 (31-50): You can be better.

- Make specific goals.
- Work on your skills.
- Give your 100% on every activity you do.
- Do the most challenging thing just after you wake up.
- Be consistent with your activities.
- Choose your battles.

Category 4 (51-70): You are underutilizing yourself.

- Tame your mind to never wander off.
- Allocate yourself specific space and time for doing the important tasks.
- Overcome self criticism.
- Improve your lifestyle choices (healthy eating, sleeping, low alcohol intake, etc.).
- Slowly and deliberately improve your social circle.

Category 5 (71-100): You are born for a better cause. Don't waste your life.

- Minimize distraction from social media.
- Keep a check on your social circle. If they are impacting you negatively, change your surroundings immediately.
- Put a check on your time thieves.
- Add a source of inspiration in your life. Start with listening to motivational videos on youtube. If you like to read, start with biographies of your favorite personalities.
- Practice growth mindset.

PART 2: 21 Days of change

We all have it tough to keep track of our daily activities. To push ourselves every day, we need to track and study our actions. This simple but effective tracker will help you follow your movements. Keep it accessible all the time. Review your performances. Challenge yourself every day and enjoy your new potential! Whenever you need to track something, take an A4 size paper. Divide it in 7*3 and start tracking. Make sure you keep it close to you.

Steps for your first tracker: 1. Write down one activity you will track today onwards. 2. Clearly specify why do you think it is necessary to track it. 3. Write down what major differences will it bring in your life. 4. Get your tracker ready.

PART 3: Be your hero

Why to look for motivation outside, when the real hero is inside? The following are a set of questions to help you tap your inner motivation. We all have a hero hidden inside us. These questions are developed to remind you of your greatness.

1. Three things you have done that you felt you could not do.

-
-
-

2. Three things which were once your weakness but are your strength now.

-
-
-

3. Three things that make you stand different from the crowd.

-
-
-

4. Three heroic things you did which fills you up with confidence and courage.

-
-
-

5. Three times you motivated others.

-
-
-

6. Three courageous things you do regularly.

-
-
-

7. Three areas where you envision yourself doing successfully in future.

-
-
-

8. Three times when you proved others wrong by outperforming your own mark.

-
-
-

PART 4: LIVING BY THE VALUES

Stephen Covey once said, "Peace of mind comes when your life is in harmony with true principles and values and in no other way." Your values define you. They distinguish you from others and act as a guiding force in your decisions. The following questions will help you in identifying the core values that resonate the most with you:

1 Three values that were always guiding you through your decisions.

-
-
-

2 Three things you would never do to someone.

-
-
-

3 Three immoral acts you did previously that you would never do in future.

-
-
-

4 Three qualities you would like to be known for?

-
-
-

5 Three values you will embed in your children.

-
-
-

6 Three things you can do forever for free.

-
-
-

7 Three past choices that made you feel proud of yourself.

-
-
-

8 Keeping in mind the above answers, what are the three values you want to embed in your life?

-
-
-

PART 5: Accountability Report

When there is no accountability, there's no responsibility. Your chances of failure reduce when there is a trustworthy critique to supervise. Getting an accountability partner will make sure that your symbiotic relationship takes you to places! The following exercise is to put your answerability to the test. Set goals together and let your partner review your performance. Have a mutual assessment and note down each other's learnings and mistakes.

Partner 1

<table>
<tr><td colspan="3" align="center">ACCOUNTABILITY REPORT</td></tr>
<tr><td></td><td></td><td>Under/Over/Well Performed</td></tr>
<tr><td>Goal 1</td><td></td><td></td></tr>
<tr><td>Goal 2</td><td></td><td></td></tr>
<tr><td>Goal 3</td><td></td><td></td></tr>
<tr><td colspan="3" align="center">Mutual Assessment:</td></tr>
<tr><td>Mistakes and Learnings</td><td></td><td></td></tr>
<tr><td>Extra Achievements</td><td></td><td></td></tr>
</table>

Partner 2

ACCOUNTABILITY REPORT		
		Under/Over/Well Performed
Goal 1		
Goal 2		
Goal 3		
Mutual Assessment:		
Mistakes and Learnings		
Extra Achievements		

PART 6: An easy mechanism to delegation

All productivity tools and time management hacks can lead you far. But eventually, there comes the point where your workload becomes unbearable. That is when the process of delegation comes in handy. Before you fill this exercise, have a thorough look at the below example:

Let's say you are a YouTuber. The core tasks a YouTuber does are-content creation, video recording, editing, marketing, and finding sponsors. Some non-core tasks would be management, hiring, managing social media profiles, finding new interesting topics, customer management, and preparing the setup.

Here's how your first draft of delegation exercise might look:

CORE TASKS OR TASKS REQUIRING CORE SKILLS	CAN BE DONE BY OTHERS	MANAGERIAL ACTIVITIES	TASKS THAT CAN BE AVOIDED
Content Creation	Finding new interesting topics	Management	Spending time on tracking other youtubers
Editing	Preparing the setup	Hiring	
Marketing		Customer management	
Finding sponsors		Managing social media profiles	
Video creation			
DO MORE	**DELEGATE IMMEDIATELY**	**MINIMISE OR DELEGATE**	**ELIMINATE OR DELEGATE**

Though the skills would be completely different for different YouTubers, let's assume that you are extremely fond of the video creation process and editing. And marketing and finding sponsors are more of a necessity for you than of a choice. Gathering information is another requisite core task to your video creation and hence you want to handle it yourself. In the present scenario, you can shift the two core activities- marketing and finding sponsors from category A to category B. Now coming to the activities listed in category C, out of the four activities listed, say you realized hiring can be done by another teammate and hence can be shifted to category B, and with some scrutiny, you found out that social media profile management isn't reaping the expected results, consuming unnecessarily time and effort, and hence can be shifted to category D

CORE TASKS OR TASKS REQUIRING CORE SKILLS	CAN BE DONE BY OTHERS	MANAGERIAL ACTIVITIES	TASKS THAT CAN BE AVOIDED
Content Creation	Finding new interesting topics	Overseeing the process	Spending time on tracking other youtubers
Editing	Preparing the setup	Customer management	
Video creation	Hiring ←	~~Hiring~~	
~~Marketing~~ →	Marketing	Managing social media profiles ←	~~Managing social media profiles~~
~~Finding sponsors~~ →	Finding sponsor		
DO MORE	**DELEGATE IMMEDIATELY**	**MINIMISE OR DELEGATE**	**ELIMINATE OR DELEGATE**

Your exercise:

CORE TASKS OR TASKS REQUIRING CORE SKILLS	CAN BE DONE BY OTHERS	MANAGERIAL ACTIVITIES	TASKS THAT CAN BE AVOIDED
DO MORE	DELEGATE IMMEDIATELY	MINIMISE OR DELEGATE	ELIMINATE OR DELEGATE

PART 7: Goal Finder

Do you have all your goals figured out? If not, this exercise will surely help you!

Instructions:

[1], [2], [3] - Write down 2 most significant goals of your life
[4] - Write down all the activities you perform on a daily basis
[5] - Write down the purpose or motivation behind each activity
[6] - Categorise entries from [5] into core and non core goals Core values are the ones that add maximum value to your life and non core goals are the ones that add little to no value in your life
[7]- The activities you have categorized as core goals in [6] are your final goals. The non alignment of goals written in [3] and [7] show that your actions and your goals aren't aligned. Either you have to change your goals or your daily activities."
[8] - Write down the extra activities you should take up to achieve your core goals
[9] - Write down the activities that are diverting you from your core goals

Purpose	Daily activities
Personal life	Family time, building relations
Recreational	hobbies, parties, fun with family
Financial goals	job, skill acquisition, education
Health and fitness	exercise, meditation, weight loss
Elevating boredom	netflix, music, social media
Necessity	socialising, attending events, household tasks

Fill it with the help of the description and examples given above:

Long term goals (15 years) [1]	Medium term goals (5 years) [2]	Short term goal (1 year) [3]
Daily Activities [4]	Purpose behind it? [5]	Categorise as core/non core goals [6]
My ultimate goals are: [7]	Task that can augment my core goals [8]	Task that are hampering my core goals [9]

PART 8: My next 3

Use "My next 3" planner to map out actions for your next three days. After three days have elapsed, visit your planner again to review your actions.

Instructions:

Things that eat up my time that I need to avoid: Write down things that reduce your productivity. It can be as simple as unnecessary socialising or watching TV or working on tasks that are not aligned with your current objectives. Ex: Window shopping with a friend, Netflix, video games, etc.

GOAL 1 and GOAL 2: Write down your top 2 objectives for the next 3 days. Keep the specifications clear and simple. Don't write because you have something on your plate. Write because you mean to do it.

Three tasks I will do in my free time: Make a list of activities that you would like to do in your free time. Do not fill this up with apparent choices like spending time with family. Instead, list down some meaningful, fun, and entertaining activities. Be specific. Example: Read- Click Reset, Watch- The Game Changers documentary, Meet- Mr. A, Podcast- Jay Shetty E7, etc.

Comments and Ratings: While reviewing it after three days, put a tick mark on the blank space in front of finished tasks. This way you can keep track of yourself. It will also make you more serious about achieving your goals. Also, think about what you could have done better. As you move ahead, practice to set stringent goals and yet achieve them.

<table>
<tr><td colspan="4" align="center">MY NEXT 3</td></tr>
<tr><td colspan="4">Things that eat up my time that I need to avoid</td></tr>
<tr><td></td><td></td><td></td><td></td></tr>
<tr><td></td><td></td><td></td><td></td></tr>
<tr><td colspan="2">GOAL 1:_________________</td><td colspan="2">GOAL 2:_________________</td></tr>
<tr><td></td><td></td><td></td><td></td></tr>
<tr><td></td><td></td><td></td><td></td></tr>
<tr><td></td><td></td><td></td><td></td></tr>
<tr><td></td><td></td><td></td><td></td></tr>
<tr><td></td><td></td><td></td><td></td></tr>
<tr><td colspan="4">Four tasks I will do in my free time</td></tr>
<tr><td></td><td></td><td></td><td></td></tr>
<tr><td></td><td></td><td></td><td></td></tr>
<tr><td colspan="2">Comments</td><td colspan="2">Ratings</td></tr>
<tr><td></td><td></td><td></td><td></td></tr>
</table>

References

CHAPTER 1

[1.1] The Hidden Messages in Water by Masaru Emoto

CHAPTER 2

[2.1] The Price of Incivility; HBR Jan-Feb,2013 issue; Christine Porath, Christine Pearson

[2.2] The Only Thing More Powerful Than Positive Thinking | by Madison Epting

[2.3] Dr. Bruce Lipton Shocked the World with his Discovery - The American Institute of Stress

[2.4] The Ship of Theseus, 50 Trillion Cells and The Importance of Purpose, Aidan McCullen, Medium The Ship of Theseus, 50 Trillion Cells and The Importance of Purpose | by Aidan McCullen | The Thursday Thought | Medium

CHAPTER 4

[4.1] Survey of US teens ages 13-17 conducted Sep 17-Nov 25, 2018, Pew Research Center

[4.2] University of Bordeaux, France, Magalie Lenoir

[4.3] Child Mortality, Melinda Gates https://datareport.goalkeepers.org/case-studies/child-mortality

CHAPTER 5

[5.1] Think like Zuck, The Five Business Secrets of Facebook's Improbably Brilliant CEO Mark Zuckerberg, Ekaterina Walter

[5.2] Elon Musk, How the billionaire CEO of SpaceX and Tesla is shaping our future, Ashlee Vance

CHAPTER 6

[6.1] Job, Veronika & Dweck, Carol & Walton, Gregory. (2010). Ego Depletion-Is It All in Your Head? Implicit Theories About Willpower Affect Self-Regulation. Psychological science. 21. 1686-93. 10.1177/0956797610384745

[6.2] The Creative Stereotype Effect, Denis Dumas, Kevin N. Dunbar

[6.3] Modulation of muscle responses evoked by transcranial magnetic stimulation during the acquisition of new fine motor skills, A. Pascual-Leone, D. Nguyet, L. G. Cohen, J. P. Brasil-Neto, A. Cammarota, and M. Hallett

CHAPTER 7

[7.1] Josh Bersin, "Becoming Irresistible: A new model for employee engagement," Deloitte Review, Issue 16, January 26, 2015.

[7.2] Culture and Values: Starbucks Coffee Company

CHAPTER 8

[8.1] Sirois, Fuschia. (2014). Procrastination and Stress: Exploring the Role of Self-compassion. Self and Identity. 13. 128-145. 10.1080/15298868.2013.763404

[8.2] Why You Procrastinate (It Has Nothing to Do With Self-Control) - The New York Times

CHAPTER 9

[9.1] Iacocca: An autobiography, by Lee Iacocca and William Novak

[9.2] Jim Kwik, 10 Brain Hacks to Learn Fast, Retain More and Forget Less, Mindvalley Free Masterclass

[9.3] Task Selection and Workload: A Focus on Completing Easy Tasks Hurts Long-Term Performance, Diwas S. KC (Emory University), Bradley R. Staats (University of North Carolina at Chapel Hill), Maryam Kouchaki (Northwestern University), Francesca Gino (Harvard Business School)

CHAPTER 10

[10.1] For Real Productivity, Less is Truly More

[10.2] Relax! You'll Be More Productive By Tony Schwartz, https://www.nytimes.com/2013/02/10/opinion/sunday/relax-youll-be-more-productive.html

[10.3] Effect of frequent interruptions of prolonged sitting on self-perceived levels of energy, mood, food cravings and cognitive function, Audrey Bergouignan, Kristina T. Legget, Nathan De Jong, Elizabeth Kealey, Janet Nikolovski, Jack L. Groppel, Chris Jordan, Raphaela O'Day, James O. Hill and Daniel H. Bessesen

CHAPTER 11

[11.1] Strang S, Hoeber C, Uhl O, et al. Impact of nutrition on social decision making. Proc Natl Acad Sci U S A. 2017;114(25):6510-6514. doi:10.1073/pnas.1620245114 https://www.ncbi.nlm.nih.gov/pmc/articles/PMC5488927/

[11.2] https://www.nytimes.com/2006/12/10/magazine/10section1C.t-1.html, https://medicine.yale.edu/news/medicineatyale/this-is-your-brain-on-an-empty-stomach/

[11.3] On Carrots and Curiosity: Eating Fruit and Vegetables Is Associated With Greater Flourishing in Daily Life, Tamlin S Conner 1 , Kate L Brookie, Aimee C Richardson, Maria A Polak, https://pubmed.ncbi.nlm.nih.gov/25080035/

[11.4] Ng, S.W., Slining, M.M., & Popkin, B.M. (2012). Use of caloric and noncaloric sweeteners in US consumer packaged foods, 2005-2009. Journal of the Academy of Nutrition and Dietetics , 112(11), 1828-1834.e1821-1826.

[11.5] U.S. Food and Drug Administration, . (2004, November). How to Understand and Use the Nutrition Facts Label. Retrieved from: https://www.fda.gov/food/new-nutrition-facts-label/how-understand-and-use-nutrition-facts-label

[11.6] University of Bordeaux, France, Magalie Lenoir

CHAPTER 12

[12.1] Crew Factors in Flight Operations IX: Effects of Planned Cockpit Rest on Crew Performance and Alertness in Long-Haul Operations, https://ntrs.nasa.gov/archive/nasa/casi.ntrs.nasa.gov/19950006379.pdf

[12.2] Sleep-dependent learning: a nap is as good as a night, Sara Mednick, Ken Nakayama & Robert Stickgold

[12.3] Take a Nap! Change your life, Sara Mednick

[12.4]   https://www.cbsnews.com/news/napping-you-snooze-you-win/

CHAPTER 14

[14.1] The digital skills gap is widening fast. Here's how to bridge it, World Economic Forum Https://www.weforum.org/agenda/2019/03/the-digital-skills-gap-is-widening-fast-here's-how-to-bridge-it/

CHAPTER 16

[16.1] Streeter CC, Whitfield TH, Owen L, et al. Effects of yoga versus walking on mood, anxiety, and brain GABA levels: a randomized controlled MRS study. J Altern Complement Med. 2010;16(11):1145-1152. doi:10.1089/acm.2010.0007

[16.2] Bokhari, S., Schneider, R.H., Salerno, J.W. et al. Effects of cardiac rehabilitation with and without meditation on myocardial blood flow using quantitative positron emission tomography: A pilot study. J. Nucl. Cardiol. (2019). https://doi.org/10.1007/s12350-019-01884-9

[16.3] Lisanne F ten Brinke LF, Bolandzadeh N, Nagamatsu LS, et alAerobic exercise increases hippocampal volume in older women with probable mild cognitive impairment: a 6-month randomized controlled trialBritish Journal of Sports Medicine 2015;49:248-254

CHAPTER 17

[17.1] Japanese workers feel guilty taking time off and use fewer holidays than their international peers: survey, Japan Times https://www.japantimes.co.jp/news/2017/12/12/national/japanese-workers-feel-guilty-taking-time-off-use-fewer-holidays-international-peers-survey/#.XvISnUBuLIU

[17.2] The Productivity Of Working Hours by John Pencavel, Stanford University 2012

[17.3] US Travel Association, Paid time off trends in the US, 2018

[17.4] https://www.sweatelite.co/the-end-of-season-rest-periods-of-the-worlds-best-athletes/#

CHAPTER 18

[18.1] Extraneous factors in judicial decisions, Shai Danziger, Jonathan Levav, and Liora Avnaim-Pesso

[18.2] Iyengar SS, Wells RE, Schwartz B. Doing better but feeling worse. Looking for the "best" job undermines satisfaction. Psychol Sci. 2006;17(2):143-150.

CHAPTER 19

[19.1] Van Dongen HP, Maislin G, Mullington JM, Dinges DF. The cumulative cost of additional wakefulness: dose-response effects on neurobehavioral functions and sleep physiology from chronic sleep restriction and total sleep deprivation [published correction appears in Sleep. 2004 Jun 15;27(4):600]. Sleep. 2003;26(2):117-126. doi:10.1093/sleep/26.2.117

[19.2] Coordinated memory replay in the visual cortex and hippocampus during sleep, Article in Nature Neuroscience, Feb 2007

[19.3] Why we sleep: Unlocking the power of sleep and dreams, Matt Walker

[19.4] Sleep inspires insight, Ullrich Wagner, Steffen Gais, Hilde Haider, Rolf Verleger & J

CHAPTER 21

[21.1] The role of deliberate practice in the acquisition of expert performance, Ericsson, K. Anders,Krampe, Ralf T.,Tesch-Römer, Clemens, Psychological Review, Vol 100(3), Jul 1993, 363-406

[21.2] The David Rubenstein Show: Marriott CEO Arne Sorenson

[21.3] The Real Leadership Lessons of Steve Jobs, Walter Issacson, April 2012 Issue, HBR https://hbr.org/2012/04/the-real-leadership-lessons-of-steve-jobs

[21.4] The Ideal Road Not Taken: The Self-Discrepancies Involved in People's Most Enduring Regrets, Shai Davidai, The New School for Social Research and Thomas Gilovich, Cornell University

CHAPTER 23

[23.1] Productivity Isn't About Time Management. It's About Attention Management., Adam Grant, New York Times https://www.nytimes.com/2019/03/28/smarter-living/productivity-isnt-about-time-management-its-about-attention-management.html?action=click&module=RelatedLinks&pgtype=Article.

[23.2] All the Charts, Tables, and Checklists You Need to Conduct Better Meetings, HBR, https://hbr.org/2015/04/all-the-charts-tables-and-checklists-you-need-to-conduct-better-meetings.

[23.3] Stop the meeting madness How to free up time for meaningful work by Leslie A. Perlow, Constance Noonan Hadley, and Eunice Eun, July–August 2017 issue (pp.62–69) of Harvard Business Review.

[23.4] Mayo Clinic

[23.5] Wings of Fire, An Autobiography of A P J Abdul Kalam (1999), former President of India, A. P. J. Abdul Kalam and Arun Tiwari

CHAPTER 24

[24.1] The David Rubenstein Show: Masayoshi Son on Bloomberg

[24.2] Deep Work, Cal Newport

CHAPTER 25

[25.1] Killingsworth, M. A., & Gilbert, D. T. (2010). A wandering mind is an unhappy mind. Science, 330, 932.

[25.2] Research by Carleton University

[25.3] NY Post

[25.4] The Telegraph

[25.5] Leroy, Sophie. (2009). Why is it so Hard to do My Work? The Challenge of Attention Residue when Switching Between Work Tasks. Organizational Behavior and Human Decision Processes. 109. 168-181. 10.1016/j.obhdp.2009.04.002.

CHAPTER 27

[27.1] Global Web Index https://blog.globalwebindex.com/chart-of-the-day/a-third-of-online-time-spent-on-social-media/

[27.2] No more FOMO: Limiting social media decreases loneliness and depression, Melissa G. Hunt, Rachel Marx, Courtney Lipson, and Jordyn Young, University of Pennsylvania, Journal of Social and Clinical Psychology, Vol. 37, No. 10, 2018, pp. 751-768

REFERENCES

[27.3] Deloitte's Global Mobile Consumer Survey, 2017: US edition